Grandfather Knows Best

Grandfather Knows Best

A Geezer's Guide to Life, Immaturity, and
Learning How to Change Diapers All Over Again

Jerry Zezima

GRANDFATHER KNOWS BEST
A GEEZER'S GUIDE TO LIFE, IMMATURITY, AND LEARNING
HOW TO CHANGE DIAPERS ALL OVER AGAIN

iUniverse books may be ordered through booksellers or by contacting:

iUniverse
1663 Liberty Drive
Bloomington, IN 47403
www.iuniverse.com
1-800-Authors (1-800-288-4677)

ISBN: 978-1-4917-8549-2 (sc)
ISBN: 978-1-4917-8550-8 (e)

Print information available on the last page.

iUniverse rev. date: 12/14/2015

Dedication

To my beautiful granddaughter, Chloe, this book is dedicated with love from Poppie.

Acknowledgments

To my family — first, foremost, and always — thanks for all of your love and support, and for putting up with my stupid jokes all these years.

To John Breunig, of my hometown paper, The Stamford Advocate, and Hearst Connecticut Media Group, thanks for running my column even though it has no redeeming social value. Thanks also to Christine Hall and Dieter Stanko for being accomplices.

To the good folks at Tribune News Service, especially Mary Elson, who recently left TNS, and Zach Finken, thanks for distributing my column to newspapers far and wide. And you wonder why journalism is in trouble.

To the National Society of Newspaper Columnists, thanks for lowering your otherwise high standards not only to accept me as a member, but to elect me president. I suspect beer was involved.

To Kim West, Emmanuel Lee, May Alvarez, and the rest of the team at iUniverse, thanks for helping to make this book a reality. I hope the publishing world will forgive you.

To anyone I may have forgotten, because I am, after all, a geezer, thanks. Now you can sleep better knowing your names are not associated with this book.

Introduction

You have to be young to be a grandfather. If you aren't, being a grandfather will make you young again.

That is what I have discovered since my granddaughter, Chloe, was born.

In three short years, Chloe has helped me recapture my youth, which admittedly isn't difficult considering I haven't grown up.

My wife, Sue, who also happens to be Chloe's grandmother, will vouch for that.

So will our younger daughter, Lauren, known to Chloe as Mommy, and her husband, Guillaume, aka Daddy.

If you want further verification that I am less mature than a toddler, you can ask our older daughter, Katie, and her husband, Dave.

They will all tell you that Chloe and I have a special bond. Maybe it's because I held her for three hours in the hospital the day after she was born, rocking her gently and telling her stupid jokes.

Whatever the reason, if I show up, no matter who else is there, she will want to come to me. Then we will run around the table, or play hide-and-seek, or just act silly.

Needless to say, but I will say it anyway, I am over the moon for this little girl.

The main reason, I am sure, is because Chloe reminds me so much of Lauren when she was that age, right down to the blond curls.

I remember the love and pride I felt — and will always feel — at being the father of two beautiful daughters who have grown up to be wonderful, talented, and well-adjusted young women, primarily because they take after their mother.

That Lauren also is a fabulous mother only adds to the pleasure.

I am happy, too, that Guillaume is such a good father, that Katie and Dave are a terrific aunt and uncle, and that Sue is the world's best grandmother.

That is why, despite my corruptive influence, Chloe will grow up to be a wonderful, talented, and well-adjusted young woman.

But I don't want it to happen too soon. If you think your kids grow up fast, wait until you have grandchildren.

Every good thing I have ever heard about being a grandparent is true and more. So I don't understand it when some people say the best thing about being a grandparent is that they can play with their grandchildren and then give them back when it's time to go home.

I love playing with Chloe, but I don't want to give her back. Fortunately, she, Lauren, and Guillaume live about half an hour away, so we can easily visit each other's houses or take trips to the ice cream store, the park, or wherever else we go to have fun, which can be anywhere.

For me, being a grandfather is one of the best things in life, but it's not the only thing, which is why I do plenty of other things that a smarter person — such as Chloe — wouldn't think of doing.

You will read all about them in this book. Each chapter begins with a grandparent-related column and continues with tales of my other adventures.

Of course, there is no greater adventure than being a husband, a father, and, now, a grandfather. It's what keeps me young.

CHAPTER 1

"How to Be a Good Grandparent"

Now that I am a grandfather, many people whose children have recently had children have asked for my brilliant advice on how to be a good grandparent. As a world-renowned expert whose granddaughter is not even two months old but is already more mature than I am, I'd be happy to comply.

For new grandparents, changing diapers is the number one concern. It's also, of course, the number two concern. But more on that later.

First, you should know that my precious little pumpkin is the most beautiful grandbaby ever born. It is important to acknowledge this and to stop thinking that your grandchild is more adorable than mine. He or she may have been the most beautiful before Chloe made her grand entrance into the world, but not anymore. Sorry, but that's just the way it is.

With that settled, here is a vital grandparenting tip: Don't brag. Nobody wants to listen to you babble on about how alert, wonderful, and beautiful your grandchild is while looking at a hundred photos you have just taken of the little cutie. Fifty photos are more than enough.

Yes, you are proud to be a grandparent, but a little humility goes a long way. You might say something like, "My grandbaby isn't as alert, wonderful, and beautiful as Jerry Zezima's, but then, whose grandchild is?"

This brings me to your interaction with the baby. As a grandparent, you will have a profound influence on your grandchild, for better (as in the case of Sue, also known as Nini) or for worse (as in the case of yours truly, also known as Poppie).

As evidence of this, I have already babysat for Chloe a few times. I fed her, changed her, and played with her. I also watched baseball and hockey

1

games with her. I even told her jokes while I held her. She looked up at me and smiled. When Lauren heard this, she said, "That was just gas."

Now we come to the crucial part: Caring for the baby. It may have been thirty years since you were last entrusted with an infant, but it will all come back to you in pungent waves of nostalgia.

As you will recall, babies do three things: sleep, eat, and poop. Nice work if you can get it.

The main difference between babies and adults is that babies not only can get away with it but are actually praised for their efforts.

"Yay!" is the typical reaction when the baby polishes off a bottle faster than you have ever chugged a beer.

"Good job!" everyone says when the baby burps.

"Way to go!" they all exclaim, coughing slightly, when the baby does his or her business.

Speaking of which, being on diaper duty is not nearly as bad as it seemed when your kids were babies. In fact, it's a refreshing change. Well, maybe not refreshing, but it's breathtakingly simple, even if it's not a good idea to breathe while cleaning up.

This helps you bond with your grandchild and is the ultimate proof of your love and devotion to the little darling.

There you have it, new grandparents. This is just a primer, and I will impart more wisdom to you as your grandchild gets older, but at least now you have the basics.

So go ahead and enjoy being a Nini or a Poppie. There's nothing like it. You can even brag a little. You can also feel free to show unsuspecting people all those pictures you just took because I know that the new addition to your family really is beautiful.

And don't forget the most important thing: Despite what anyone says, when your adorable little grandbaby smiles at you, it's not necessarily gas.

"The Big Six-Oh"

According to an age-old maxim that has never appeared in Maxim, the racy men's magazine whose target audience is not exactly geezers like me, age is relative, especially if you have old relatives.

I am one of the oldest relatives in my family, not counting those who are dead, and recently proved it by reaching the ripe old age of sixty. In fact, I was so ripe that I had to take a shower.

Because I have passed this milestone, which is better than passing a kidney stone, I am offering some pearls of wisdom to all you people who are younger than I am, which these days is just about everybody. Those few who are actually older either don't need my wisdom or do but will promptly forget it.

Here is the first pearl, which I got at a pawnshop: Wisdom comes too late in life to be useful to you and is best passed on to your children, who aren't wise enough to realize that you finally know what you're talking about.

As Katie and Lauren will swear, and not even under oath, I have never known what I was talking about, so what's the point in starting now?

A lot of people my age say they don't want to be a burden to their children. Not me. Being a burden is my goal.

Fortunately, my kids don't have to worry just yet because sixty is the new fifty. Or maybe even the new forty. At least that's what baby boomers believe. As a boomer who is bad at math (and has the checkbook to prove it), I think this makes perfect sense.

I have had people tell me (because I have asked them to) that I don't look sixty. Each time, I have responded: "You mean I look even older? I must be having a bad face day."

These people will invariably smile and say, "No, you look younger." Then they will make some lame excuse about being late for a root canal and walk swiftly away.

Still, this is the best time of life because you can do everything you have always done, but if there is something you don't want to do, you can pull the age card.

"I don't think I should be shoveling snow anymore," you might say to no one in particular, because no one in particular will listen to you.

Or, "I don't think I should be lugging furniture anymore."

Or, "I *do* think I should be lying in a hammock with a beer."

This last one may not work, especially on a nice summer day when you really ought to be doing something that won't give you a heart attack, like cutting the grass, but it's worth trying anyway.

Here's another pearl: Exercise and health food will kill you. Eat what you want because at some point in your life, someone will discover that the supposedly good things you have been eating for so long are now bad for you and that the bad things are really pretty good after all. And for God's sake, don't take up running because you will be hit by a car driven by either a young maniac who is texting or a little old man who can't see over the steering wheel.

Speaking of driving, you can't do it if you don't know where you put your car keys. Check your right pocket. If they're not there, look on the kitchen counter.

Here is the last pearl, which I plan to give to Sue before the cops find out it's missing: Never grow up. I have lived so long because I am shockingly immature, which makes me feel young.

Sue, who is the same age and is as beautiful as ever, is the real reason for my longevity. If it weren't for her, I would be either dead or in prison.

So enjoy life, fellow sexagenarians, don't forget where you put your car keys, and know that there are plenty of good times ahead.

"The Pun and Only"

As a guy who has always loved puns, and has been known to use as many as ten at a time (even if they don't work, I can say, "No pun in ten did"), I had long looked for a venue where my wordplay would be ear relevant.

That's why I was happy as a clam, I will admit for shellfish reasons, to find out about Punderdome 3000, a monthly contest for people who have grown to love puns and audience members who have groaned to hear them.

Punderdome is the brainchild of entrepreneurial comic Fred Firestone and his real child, funny daughter Jo, who together, if you consider their surname, are two tires, though fortunately they are not too tired to put on a great show.

The latest one was held, as usual, at Littlefield, a fabulous performance and art space in Brooklyn, where a tree grows because that's where the Tree Stooges grew up.

I signed up, showed up, and found myself in a crowd of about four hundred young, happy, and friendly people who were so eclectic that they must have paid the eclectic bill and so hip that I, clearly the oldest among them, figured I'd need a hip replacement.

I also was one of seventeen contestants, who included individuals and two-person teams, which brought the total number of participants to about two dozen if you add them up, though you shouldn't divide them, especially if you are division-impaired.

When I registered with Jo in the Littlefield lobby, I had to pick a punny nickname, so I selected JZ because, I said initially, "They're my initials."

Fred and Jo took the stage (and gave it back) to explain the rules: Contestants would be given a topic and have a minute and a half to prepare. They would then be called up to a microphone and have two minutes to be off and punning.

Their scores would be registered on a "human clap-o-meter," on a scale of one (lowest) to ten (highest), based on the reaction of the crowd.

The first round was divided into three parts. My group, composed of six contestants, went last. The topic: sea creatures.

After the first contestant went, I stepped up to the microphone and said, "Before we started, he and I decided to swap puns. It was a squid pro quo."

The crowd went wild. "Your applause is so loud," I continued, holding my hand to my head, "I have a haddock."

I rattled off a stream of sea-creature puns. As my two minutes ended, I said, "Everything I said up here was on porpoise."

I got thunderous applause that registered at 9.5 and, along with two other punsters in my group, made the first cut.

The second round's topic: yoga. Since I don't do yoga, it was, I said, "a stretch," but after saying that the practice was invented by a famous baseball player, "Yoga Berra," I scored a ten and went on, with three other contestants, to the semifinals.

The topic: the names of people you went to high school with.

I said I went to high school so long ago that many of the boys in my class became Founding Fathers. "Then there was the guy who became big in coffee: Joe. And the girl who became a lawyer: Sue."

I ended by saying that I went to college at Pun State.

My score: Ten. I was in the finals! It was me against One-Two Punch, a team of two bright and funny young guys, Dylan DePice, twenty-six, and Noah Berg, twenty-four. There was no preparation time. We would stand at separate microphones and, for four minutes, volley puns. The topic: babies.

"My little granddaughter is so smart, she's studying Shakespeare," I began. "The other day I heard her say, 'To pee or not to pee, that is the question.'"

This gave birth to a series of infantile comments ("We're in a womb with a view") that whipped the crowd into a frenzy.

My score: Ten. I won! I was Punderdome champ.

My prize: a chocolate fountain and fondue maker. I brought it home to Sue, who has had to put up with my puns all these years. It was the least I could fondue.

"Scents and Sensibility"

For three decades, my loyal, intelligent, and, let's face it, masochistic readers have said that I stink. This time, they're right.

That's because, in a display of gluttony that did not, unfortunately, take my breath away, I participated in a garlic-eating contest.

This pungent event was the highlight of the Long Island Garlic Festival, which was held at Garden of Eve Organic Farm and Market in Riverhead, New York.

As about a hundred people crammed into a tent to get a whiff of the competition, which should have put the smell of fear in them but instead produced an air redolent with excitement, I stood at a long table with seven other contestants, all of whom could sniff victory and, more important from a dollars-and-scents perspective, the $100 grand prize.

"Did you practice?" asked Vanessa Hagerbaumer, an event planner who was the MC for the contest.

"No," I said. "I figured nobody would want to come near me. Then again, if I started training this morning, I might have won by default."

"That would have been a good strategy," said Vanessa, who introduced the contestants and explained the rules: We would have two minutes to chew and swallow as many cloves of garlic as we could stomach. We could drink water to wash down what we ate. No spitting out or regurgitating garlic during the competition. A clove in the mouth as time ran out would be counted. Garden of Eve would not be responsible if we repulsed loved ones when we got home.

"Ready?" Vanessa said.

The crowd was breathless.

"Set."

For the last time that day, so was I.

"Go!"

I popped a clove of garlic in my mouth and started chomping. I decided not to waste time by peeling off the husk, part of which got stuck in my teeth. The rest, along with the masticated clove, went down my gullet.

A split second later, I felt like a fire extinguisher had been set off in my mouth. The intense sensation blasted out my nose, eyes and ears. Undeterred, I ate another clove. Then another.

The onlookers, who probably could have used gas masks, were going wild.

Suddenly, it was over. I had inhaled thirteen cloves of garlic.

I didn't even come close to winning. That honor went to defending champion Mark Lucas, a high school art teacher and drama director who gobbled twenty-two cloves. His secret: "I used the palm of my hand to smash them on the table, then I just swallowed them."

"I bet your students will pay attention to you tomorrow," I said.

"If they don't go home sick," Mark replied.

His victory last year was not without consequence.

"I went to a party afterward," Mark said. "A pregnant woman got nauseous, so I had to leave."

A similar fate awaited me when I got home.

"Whew!" Sue exclaimed when I walked in the door. "I could smell you coming."

She had anticipated my odoriferous condition and bought a lemon, which I sliced and sucked on.

"Any better?" I asked, exhaling toward Sue.

"No!" she cried. "It's coming out your pores."

I chewed on some mint from Sue's garden.

"You still leave a backdraft when you walk by," she said, fanning her nose with her hand.

Finally, I tried a tomato.

"Tomato juice is used on dogs when they get sprayed by skunks," I noted.

"Even a skunk would smell better than you do," said Sue.

The tomato didn't do the trick, either. What might have helped was $100 worth of breath mints, but since I didn't win, I couldn't afford them.

My only consolation was that I got an "I Love Garlic" T-shirt. It was the only thing about me that didn't stink.

"Sleeping My Way to the Top"

As a dedicated employee who has often been accused of sleeping on the job (I seldom hear the accusations because I am, of course, asleep), I knew

7

it was a dream come true when I found a job on which I would actually be required to sleep.

I refer to a position (horizontal) with the impressive title of snooze director, which opened up at Sleepy's, the mattress company that doesn't rest on its laurels when it comes to giving people a good night's sleep.

Emily Barrett, twenty-five, was hired as Sleepy's first snooze director but left the company a couple of months ago to become a production assistant for MTV. When I read that the job was open, I applied. Then I took a nap so I would be refreshed and coherent enough to make a good impression.

I did just that when I went to Sleepy's headquarters in Hicksville, New York, for an interview with marketing manager Andrew Jedlicka, who asked why I thought I was qualified to be the new snooze director.

"I was born for this job," I told him. "In fact, I was born more than three weeks past my due date. My mother later said that I was sleeping happily and didn't want to come out. Also, I have a lot of experience because I'm a geezer who has been sleeping for decades. And I'm a newspaper columnist whose work frequently puts people to sleep."

Then I told Jedlicka about the message on my answering machine at work: "Hi, this is Jerry Zezima. I'm either away from my desk or at my desk but fast asleep. Please leave a message and I'll get back to you."

"Those are excellent qualifications," Jedlicka acknowledged. "What if we made you an offer?"

I yawned and replied, "I'd have to sleep on it."

The interview went so well that I was called back for the decisive round at the Sleepy's store in New York City, where I learned that I was one of five finalists out of seventy applicants.

The other four finalists were women in their twenties.

Unlike the first interview, this one was recorded by a camera crew. I repeated my spiel (now it can be used as a cure for insomnia) and emphasized the health benefits of a good night's sleep — especially, I added with a wink, on a quality mattress. And I said I knew that the job of snooze director entailed more than snoozing. I would have to stay awake long enough to make appearances at Sleepy's stores and talk to the public about the restorative effects of sleep.

I also performed the "pillow test," in which I explained how to tell if you have a good pillow (it should snap back to its original position after being folded in half, preferably not with your head on it); demonstrated my nightly sleeping positions (none vertical); and stressed the importance of lying on the proper side of the mattress (the top).

Though I performed well, I lost out to Elizabeth Murphy, twenty-five, of Floral Park, New York, Sleepy's smart and personable new snooze director.

"I'm very excited," Murphy told me over the phone after the decision had been announced a week later. "I think my ability to talk to people helped. It's also a good thing I'm a morning person, since the interview was before lunch."

Murphy added that she sleeps with Daisy, her fifty-pound beagle, who is an even better sleeper than she is. "It's conceivable that Daisy could have gotten the job," said Murphy.

"We loved Elizabeth's energy," explained Jeff Lobb, chief marketing officer for Sleepy's. "But we loved you, too. You made a compelling case, with all your sleeping experience and the fact that you're a writer who helps others fall asleep. Still, we felt that Elizabeth was the right choice. I hope you're not too disappointed."

"Don't worry," I said. "I won't lose any sleep over it."

CHAPTER 2

"Grumpy's Guide to Grandparenting"

When Chloe was born three months ago, I thought I knew everything there was to know about being a grandfather but was afraid to ask.

Then, flush with triumph after changing a diaper, I got over my fear and asked for pearls of wisdom from my college buddy and longtime friend Tim Lovelette, who has three granddaughters.

"One of the most important things you can do when you have granddaughters," said Tim, who lives on Cape Cod, Massachusetts, "is to get them to watch the Three Stooges. This is the difference between being a grandfather and being a grandmother. Men love the Stooges and women hate them. Women are missing out on a huge piece of culture. So it's crucial that we get the next generation of women — our granddaughters — to watch the Stooges. Have a Stooge marathon. Your granddaughter will love it. Then she'll be hooked. And it will be too late for her grandmother to do anything about it."

Tim added that his wife, Jane, is the best grandmother in the world, despite not being a Three Stooges fan.

"I'll put my wife up against any other grandmother," he said proudly. "We'll have a competition. They can duke it out and Jane will win."

I told Tim that Sue is a wonderful grandmother.

"I don't doubt that," he said. "But Jane has a height advantage. And Sue doesn't have Jane's experience."

That's because Tim and Jane's oldest granddaughter is six years old, the middle one is a year old, and the youngest is eight months.

"Jane watches one on Mondays and another one on Thursdays," Tim said. "She'll take the bus into Boston to babysit the youngest one and come back at night. And Jane watched the oldest one before the little girl got big enough to go to school. The most impressive thing is that Jane has to babysit me. I'm less mature than any of them."

As a result, Tim said, very little is expected of him.

"Jane assumes all the grandparenting responsibilities," he noted. "Nobody expects me to do anything. I'm not responsible by design. It's a conscious irresponsibility. I run a successful insurance business, I keep out of jail, I'm the same guy you met in college — a little heavier but even more handsome — but I've developed this aura of irresponsibility. If you start out with low expectations, you can't go wrong. That way, if you do something good, like go for a walk with your granddaughter, you can be a real hero."

"Chloe is too young to walk," I said, "but I've put her in the stroller and taken her for a spin around the patio."

"You're a good grandfather," said Tim. "I'm impressed. I'm in awe. I mean, you even change diapers."

"I guess I'm a late bloomer," I said, "because I didn't change a lot of diapers when Katie and Lauren were babies."

"I've changed one diaper in my life," Tim acknowledged. "You're willing to do things that I won't do. I love being a grandfather, and I love my granddaughters, but there's a limit to everything."

Tim does take credit for being diplomatic.

"You have to be very judicious when you have more than one granddaughter," said Tim, whose daughter-in-law is the mom of the oldest two and whose daughter is the mom of the youngest. "If one mother senses a child is getting more praise than another, it's Armageddon."

Tim said choosing the name you want your grandchildren to call you also is important.

"I like the names you and Sue picked out: Poppie and Nini," said Tim. "I've always been Big Daddy and Jane has been Go-Go. But when the youngest one was born, my daughter said she didn't like those names and wanted us to change them. So now we're Grumpy and Grammy."

Tim paused and added: "I'm Grumpy. And pretty soon, I'm going to introduce her to the Three Stooges."

"Skate Expectations"

With apologies to J.R.R. Tolkien, whose fantastic writings did not, for some reason, include a story about roller derby, I am the lord of the rink.

Or I would have been if I had been able to stand on skates long enough to be a roller derby queen.

That was my goal when I went to World Gym in East Setauket, New York, to try out for the Strong Island Derby Revolution, a women's flat-track roller derby league whose travel team competes against squads from New York, New Jersey, and Connecticut.

I signed up for the recruiting session because, even though I am a guy and would not be eligible to play, I have a feminine side. Unfortunately, that's the side I frequently landed on, a more compelling reason why I wasn't eligible to play.

I should have known I wouldn't be able to keep up with the women who tried out because I had never been on roller skates, I am old, and I am pathetically out of shape.

That didn't stop Kristi Altieri-Smith, the Revolution's head of public relations and one of the league's best players, from welcoming me to the tryout.

"We would love for you to attend," Kristi wrote in an email, which she signed with her roller derby nickname: Bite-Size Brawler.

When I arrived at the rink, I picked my own roller derby nickname: Average-Size Geezer.

Julie Dekom, who co-founded the Revolution in 2011 and is known as Wreck'em Deck'em, liked my nickname so much that she wrote it on a piece of white tape that she stuck on my black helmet, part of the mandatory equipment that included knee and elbow pads and, of course, roller skates.

After putting on my size elevens, which were kindly provided by the league, I took one step and down I went. After several more spectacular spills, Diane White, also known as Doc Block, said, "You're falling better."

I replied, "I turned the other cheek."

Diane admitted, "I'm not a real doctor — I got my nickname from a character in 'Grindhouse' — but I play one in roller derby."

She wasn't skating because she recently needed the services of a real doctor for such foot problems as tendinitis and plantar fasciitis. She also once tore a rotator cuff.

Julie sustained a trimalleolar fracture but has fully recovered and is back in action. "They put some titanium screws in my ankle," she said matter-of-factly.

Injuries are part of the game. But these roller derby players are real athletes, which is more than I can say for myself. That's why I didn't join the action in the center of the rink. I figured I would fall — this time on my face — and be run over by so many roller skate wheels that I would end up as flat as a pepperoni pizza, though not nearly as appetizing.

The women in the league pay a fee to play. Their bouts, which regularly draw hundreds of fans, have raised money for charitable causes such as the Wounded Warrior Project and the Suffolk County Coalition Against Domestic Violence. And they come from all walks (or rolls) of life.

"We have doctors, lawyers, women from diverse backgrounds," said Julie, who works as a processor for a financial group and has three children. "A lot of us are moms. We even have a couple of grandmothers."

"I'm a new grandpa," I said.

"Congratulations!" Julie said. "You'd fit right in."

"Even though I can barely stand up?" I asked.

"You're doing much better," Julie noted. "A couple more days on skates and you'll be a pro."

"Call it feminine intuition," I said, "but I'll never be a roller derby queen."

"Mighty Jerry Has Struck Out"

If you don't see me at the ballpark, hitting baseballs over the fence and signing autographs for adoring fans, it will be because I was recently on steroids, which unfortunately did nothing to help me hit baseballs over the fence and explains why nobody wants my autograph.

My dream of making it to the big leagues began when a sore throat put me on the disabled list. So I went to Stat-Health, a walk-in clinic in Port Jefferson Station, New York, and sat down with enough people to fill the bleachers at Fenway Park. All that was missing was a guy selling beer, which would have helped my throat considerably.

Instead, I saw the next best person, Dr. Richard Goldstein, who looked at my throat and said, "It's really inflamed. I am going to give you a strep test."

"Strip?" I asked, indicating that my ears were affected, too. "You mean I have to take my clothes off?"

"No," said Dr. Goldstein. "I am going to take a culture."

"The only culture I have comes from yogurt," I informed him, adding that my throat was so sore that I almost couldn't talk, gratifying my family and friends.

"You don't have strep," Dr. Goldstein said when the test results came back a few minutes later.

"I guess it's true that when it comes to being sick, men are babies," I said.

"Yes, we are," Dr. Goldstein acknowledged. "But don't worry, I won't tell anyone. It's part of our doctor-patient confidentiality. Still, I want to get rid of the inflammation in your throat, so I am going to prescribe steroids."

"There goes my baseball career," I told Dr. Goldstein, who also prescribed antibiotics, which I had to take after I finished the steroids.

I was on steroids for six days. I didn't feel any stronger, maybe because my idea of weightlifting is doing twelve-ounce curls, but I wondered if the steroids could help me hit a baseball, something I hadn't done with any regularity since Little League. And even then, half a century ago, I was terrible.

To find out, I went to Matt Guiliano's Play Like a Pro, an indoor hitting and pitching facility in nearby Hauppauge.

One of the staffers, Chris Ingram, twenty, who has played college ball as a pitcher and an outfielder at Rensselaer Polytechnic Institute in Troy, New York, and hopes to make it to the big leagues, led me to a batting cage.

"I don't think the steroids you're taking are the same ones that guys like Alex Rodriguez have used," said Ingram, who added that he has never taken them and never would.

"Cheaters shouldn't prosper, which is why I don't want to be like A-Rod," I said, noting that I would be known as J-Zez. "But I wouldn't mind having his bank account."

After I picked out a bat and put on a helmet, Ingram asked, "Do you want me to set the pitching machine on fast, medium or slow?"

"What's slow?" I replied.

"Forty-five miles per hour," said Ingram, pointing out that the speed is about half of what the average major-league pitcher throws.

"Let's go slow," I said, stepping up to the plate and waiting for the first pitch, which whizzed past me before I was even halfway through my swing.

Except for a couple of foul balls, I hit only one of sixteen pitches. And it wouldn't have come close to being a home run.

"Maybe a grounder to short," Ingram said.

For the next batch of pitches, I tried batting from the left side. I had a more natural swing, Ingram said, but it didn't help because I whiffed on all but one, which I fouled off.

"The steroids didn't work," I said afterward.

"How's your throat?" Ingram asked.

"Much better," I replied. "The soreness is gone."

"Then they did work," he said.

"Now I can go to the ballpark," I said. "If I can afford a ticket, I'll sit in the bleachers."

"Par for the Course"

As a guy who has always loved Mark Twain's definition of golf as "a good walk spoiled," I had never aspired to be the next Tiger Woods, either on or off the course, which is why I'm not rich but am, fortunately, still married.

But lately, at the ripe old age of sixty, I have had a hankering to take up the sport, which is more sensible than tennis because in golf you don't have to run after the ball. In fact, you can use a cart, which is fine on a golf course but would be kind of clunky on a tennis court.

So I went to the Bergen Point Golf Course, a beautiful waterside public course in West Babylon, New York, for a lesson with instructor Kevin Lisi.

"You've never played golf before?" asked Kevin, who is twenty-three and has been playing since he was a kid, which to me he still is.

"No," I replied. "But if Tiger Woods could win the Masters at twenty-one, and Jordan Spieth could almost win this year at twenty, the opposite could happen and a geezer like me could win. Then I could sign my AARP card and get a green jacket."

"Show me how you think a golf club should be held," said Kevin, who handed me a pitching wedge on the driving range, where I was among about a dozen people in the group lesson.

"I'm guessing this isn't the right way," I said as I grabbed the club by the head.

"You really are new at this," said Kevin, who nonetheless was impressed when I wrapped my fingers around the handle and, with a little guidance, held the club correctly. After showing me how to plant my feet, bend my back and knees, and angle the head of the club, Kevin said, "Now take a practice swing."

I raised the club parallel to the ground and lifted the head a bit higher, then brought it back down and followed through beautifully, a fluid motion that would have impressed Ben Hogan had the legendary golf champion, known for his perfect swing, not been currently deceased.

"Very good," Kevin said. "Now let's see if you can hit a ball."

I lined up the little white sphere and drove it about ninety yards.

"Are you sure you've never played golf before?" asked Kevin.

"Just miniature golf," I replied. "My kids beat me."

I drove my second shot the same distance.

"Do you think I can win the Masters?" I asked.

"You're just getting started," Kevin cautioned. "Golf's addictive, but it's a tough game."

He wasn't kidding, because those two shots were my best of the day. I steadily regressed, with some of my worst shots dribbling off the mat. Kevin was wonderful, treating me with kid gloves (or, rather, golf gloves) and trying to get me back in my original groove when he wasn't giving pointers to the other newbies.

When the hourlong lesson was over, Kevin said, "You're not bad. You just need to practice."

Later, in the pro shop, head pro Paul Rollo, who saw me on the driving range, said, "The basic principle is to move the ball forward. If it moves in the direction you want it to go, you're doing OK."

Pro shop employee Ken Klevitz added, "If you see water in front of you, forget it."

Bob Miller, director of the Bergen Point Golf Course, ambled in with his dog, a five-year-old black Lab named Lucas.

"Are you a dogleg right?" I asked Lucas.

"He's a scratch golfer," said Kevin.

"He does a lot of scratching," Bob noted. "And he scares away the geese."

"I'd be good at that," I said. "Maybe I could do it at the Masters."

"Sure," said Paul. "But if you want a green jacket, you may have to buy it yourself."

"Rocky Mountain Guy"

I have long been told, by people too numerous to mention, including members of my own family, to take a hike. But because of the rarefied air between my ears, I waited until a recent trip to the Rocky Mountains to take them up — way up — on their suggestion.

My initial ascent of a slope high enough to let me see what flight attendants were serving on passing airplanes was made during a long weekend in Granby, Colorado, a picturesque town that is about 8,000 feet above sea level. Considering I am six feet tall and live close to the shore, it is 7,994 feet higher than what I am used to.

Accompanying me on this exhausting excursion were Sue, Katie, Lauren, Dave, and Sue's brother's daughter, Ashley. All are in better shape than I am. So are some dead people, but I didn't want to join them by falling off a cliff or being eaten by a mountain lion.

The first hikers we encountered on the trail were three young children, two women who apparently were their mothers, and a white-haired lady whose age, I would estimate, was a hundred and twelve. She had a walking stick.

"Good morning!" she chirped as we tramped by. "Are you enjoying your hike?"

"This is my first one," I told her.

The lady looked at my ratty sneakers, worn sweatpants, "I Love Garlic" T-shirt, and bloodshot eyes and said, "I hope you don't have trouble with the altitude."

"I'm naturally lightheaded," I replied, "so it doesn't bother me."

What did bother me was the prospect of being attacked by any number of ferocious fauna, including but not limited to Bigfoot.

"What happens if we encounter a bear?" Sue asked.

"It would be pretty grizzly," I said.

To which Ashley responded, "Good one!"

Then there were beavers, which came to my boggled mind when we passed a stream that had been dammed by the industrious rodents.

"Last year," I recalled, "a fisherman in Europe was killed by a berserk beaver."

Dave saw the bright side when he pointed to the sparkling water and said, "Every delicious ounce of Coors Light starts right here."

I could have used a beer because I was hot on the trail (of what, I wasn't sure), but all I had was a bottle of water, and it was warm.

As we made our way up the steep grade (I was expecting my grade to be F, which would have stood for "fainted"), I actually felt invigorated.

"You're doing very well," Katie said with a touch of astonishment.

"I thought you would have keeled over by now," Lauren added optimistically.

Aside from a couple of brief rest stops, we made a beeline (and did not, fortunately, get stung by bees) to the top of the trail, where I beheld two wondrous sights: a waterfall and a lawyer.

The former was not exactly Niagara Falls, though I did approach it step by step, inch by inch, but the latter was exactly what I didn't expect to see.

"You think you can get away from us," said Patrick Fitz-Gerald, an attorney from Denver. "But we're everywhere."

He was hiking with his wife, Katie; their daughter, Larkin, three; and their golden retriever, Buddy, seven, who Patrick said is on the cover of the paperback edition of the best-selling Garth Stein novel, "Racing in the Rain."

When Patrick told me that he used to be a journalist but quit to become a lawyer, I said, "You finally found honest work."

"If you get hurt on the trail and need representation," Patrick said, "call me."

Except for a scratch on my middle finger, which I was too polite to show him, I didn't get hurt at all. On the way down, which admittedly was a lot easier than going up, I told our merry band that I had a terrific time on my first hike.

"I guess," said Lauren, speaking for everyone, "you're not over the hill after all."

CHAPTER 3

"The Prince and the Poppie"

Prince Charles
Clarence House
London SW1A 1BA
United Kingdom

Sir:

From one new grandpa to another, I am writing to congratulate you on the birth of your first grandchild. I know he is a prince of a boy because my granddaughter, who was born in March, is my little princess. I guess that makes us a couple of lucky guys who will always give our grandchildren, if you will pardon the expression, the royal treatment.

Despite our differences (you have a real job, whereas I am a public nuisance), we have much in common, even though I am a commoner who has very little common sense, which is commoner these days than you might think.

Anyway, my younger daughter and her husband (the proud new parents) were married in France the day after your older son and his wife (ditto) were married in England in 2011.

I wrote the duke and duchess a letter to congratulate them on their nuptials and to thank them for being the opening act for the wedding of the century, in which I was, of course, the father of the bride. I also noted that our happy couple had a second ceremony here in the United States, which was one more than the duke and duchess had, but who's counting?

I received a lovely reply from Mrs. Claudia Holloway, who as you know is the head of correspondence for the royal family. She wrote on behalf of the duke and duchess to extend their thanks for my good wishes and their congratulations to their fellow newlyweds.

It showed the class for which your family (and everyone in mine except, unfortunately, yours truly) is known.

In that spirit, I will not get into one-upmanship by saying that in addition to having two weddings, my daughter had a baby before your daughter-in-law did. I will say, however, that they are wonderful young women (and their husbands are wonderful young men) and that their babies — our grandchildren — are beautiful.

Now here is the most amazing thing we have in common: Both babies were born at 4:24 p.m.

It seems like they were made for each other. This, I believe, is more than just a coincidence. There must be some cosmic or divine plan at work here. Since your grandson is a prince and my granddaughter is a princess, their lives seem destined to intertwine.

Could there be a wedding (or two) in our future?

You never know. But here at the Zezimanse, as we call our family home, we are very excited at the prospect.

First, though, your grandson will have to prove himself worthy of my granddaughter, which, considering his lineage, I have no doubt he will do.

When he gets a bit older, he will have to hold his bottle (ba-ba in baby talk) the proper way, with his pinkies up. And he will have to know which plastic fork to use when he begins eating solid food, which initially will consist of mashed peas and carrots. I hear they are better than a lot of British meals, but I don't want to be a culinary critic.

I merely want to say that this could be the beginning of a beautiful relationship.

I also want to say that we should enjoy being grandfathers. There is, as I am sure you have already found out, nothing like it. I'm also sure that you have pampered your grandson, though I don't know if you have Pampered him. If not, you really should lend a hand. In fact, two hands. Just make sure you are not wearing white gloves.

Again, Charles, congratulations. Please give our best to your family. And let's set up a play date.

Sincerely,
Jerry Zezima

"Self-Maid Man"

I could never see myself in a little French maid's outfit, except on weekends while doing my household chores, and I don't suppose I'll ever wear one because: (a) I probably couldn't find something like that in my size and (b) I don't speak French.

But that didn't stop me from becoming a maid when I joined a team from The Maids, a national house cleaning service, and helped clean my own house.

I wasn't required to wear a little French maid's outfit — a yellow Maids polo shirt and a pair of khakis composed the official attire — but I did have to work hard to get all the dirt and dust off floors and out of corners so the house would be, as it often isn't after I am done with my chores, spotless.

I called The Maids because a husband's work is never done and, in nearly thirty-five years of marriage, I have improved my vacuuming, scrubbing, and dusting skills to the point where I wondered if I were good enough to be a professional.

"We'll find out," said Ken Quenstedt, who owns The Maids franchise that serves northwestern Suffolk County, New York, where I live.

Ken came over in a yellow Maids car with four team members: Maria, Mayra, Melanie, and Ingris. They were soon joined by Jenny, the field supervisor.

Sue, who keeps a clean house despite my help, served as the domestic supervisor.

"Jerry didn't know how to work the washing machine until a few years ago," Sue told Ken. "But he's a lot better at chores than he used to be."

"I'm best at ironing," I bragged, "because I'm a member of the press."

"Vacuuming is my specialty," said Ken, like me an empty nester whose wife appreciates his (not always superlative) efforts around the house.

I thought I was pretty good at it, too, but neither Ken nor I had anything on Maria, who had a space-age vacuum cleaner strapped to her back. It looked like a scuba tank, from which extended a hose with an attachment that Maria expertly maneuvered over the carpeting, along the ceiling, and around corners.

"May I try it?" I asked Maria, who graciously helped me strap on the vacuum and showed me how to operate it without getting entangled in the cord, which I did anyway.

"You're doing a good job," she said.

I did an even better job of dusting after watching Ingris, the team leader, deftly use her dust cloth on the bureaus and nightstands in the master bedroom.

"I usually dust around things," I confessed.

"You have to move them," said Ingris, who was impressed when I followed instructions and did the job right.

"Could I be part of the team?" I asked.

"Yes!" she answered.

Jenny was impressed with my toilet-cleaning prowess after showing me how to correctly use a brush in the porcelain convenience.

"Very good," she declared.

I was flush with excitement. It was my turn to be impressed after watching Melanie scrub down the tile in another bathroom until it was immaculate.

When I noticed that the team members were wearing shoe covers, Mayra explained, "We don't want to bring dirt into the house."

"My feet are so big," I said, "I should wear garbage bags."

Instead, the foursome used garbage bags for, yes, garbage, which they emptied out of wastebaskets.

After an hour and a half, they were finished.

"The house has never looked so clean!" Sue exclaimed.

I thanked the hardworking crew for a magnificent job and told Ken that they inspired me to be an even better house cleaner.

"Whenever you do chores," he suggested, "you can wear the yellow shirt."

"At least," I said with a sigh of relief, "I won't have to wear a little French maid's outfit."

"A Chore Thing"

The late, great humorist Erma Bombeck once said, "Housework, if you do it right, can kill you."

Since I am still alive, thanks to Sue, who does most of the housework in our house, I guess I am not doing it right.

This does not come as a surprise to either me or Sue because of a startling statistic I read in the Old Farmer's Almanac, which states: "The average American woman will spend six years of her life doing housework; the average American man, three years, eight months."

Looking on the bright side, men die sooner. According to the Almanac, the average American man lives for 76.19 years; the average American woman, 81.17 years.

This means, I figured out when I should have been doing housework, that women live about five years longer than men but do housework only two years, four months longer. So men actually do housework for a greater percentage of their lives, 21.16 vs. 13.53, than women.

"That's a stupid statistic," Sue said when she heard this, resisting the urge to end my life about sixteen years short of the average. "I've been doing housework for thirty-six years. I started the day we got married."

"No, you didn't, because we went on our honeymoon, remember?" I pointed out helpfully.

"OK, so I got a week off," Sue said. "But I've been doing housework ever since."

"You can't say I haven't helped," I said.

"Yes, you have," Sue acknowledged. "You do clean our bathroom, but I do the other two. So that means I clean twice as many bathrooms as you do."

"One and a half," I noted, reminding her that we have a half-bathroom downstairs.

Sue also acknowledged that I clean the litter boxes (for our two cats, not me, because I use the bathroom that I clean) and that I vacuum (the carpets, not the litter boxes).

"And I iron," I said, "because I'm hot stuff."

Sue ignored the remark, even though she was steamed, and added, "And you do fold clothes."

This gave her a chance to air my dirty laundry. For the first twenty-five years of our marriage, I didn't do the laundry. Then, finally, I learned how. But we recently got rid of our old washer and bought a new one, which Sue won't let me use.

"I'm afraid you'll break it," she said.

"Does this mean I don't have to do the laundry for the next twenty-five years?" I asked.

Sue looked at me as if to say, "If we're still married twenty-five years from now, I'm going to stick my head in the oven."

Speaking of which, she said, "You don't cook. And you don't empty the dishwasher. And you don't dust."

"You're not supposed to dust dishes, are you?" I inquired.

"And," Sue continued, "you don't do windows."

"That's because they're a pane," I reasoned.

Sue reminded me that I don't do yard work anymore because we hired a landscaper this year. "So you should have more time to do housework," she said.

She was right, of course, so I said, "What do you want me to do?"

"The windows," Sue responded. "They're filthy."

"Should I use ammonia and water?" I asked.

"You sound like you're stuck in the 1950s," Sue said. "Nobody uses ammonia and water anymore. Use Windex."

"I use that on the bathroom mirror," I said, though I was afraid to mention that I also use it to clean stains from the carpet when one of the cats coughs up a hairball.

I got a roll of paper towels and a bottle of Windex and proceeded to do the windows in the family room. I also cleaned the glass in the front storm door. For the first time in ages, sunshine streamed in.

"Nice job," Sue said.

"Anything to help," I replied. "Do you want me to make dinner?"

"No!" Sue shrieked. "You might burn the house down."

"At least then," I said, "we wouldn't have to clean it."

"A Glass Act"

I do windows. Unfortunately, I do them every couple of years, which gives the windows plenty of time to get dirty, and even then it is clear that I don't do them very well because I have always considered the job a pane in the glass.

This year, I let a professional end my losing streak, which was, of course, in each window.

Enter (through the front door, not a window) David Wright, owner of Mr. Wright's Window Cleaning of Centerport, New York.

Not to be confused with the New York Mets slugger of the same name ("He doesn't do windows as well as I do, but I can't hit a baseball as well as he can"), Wright was a lawyer, a financial analyst, and a monk before devoting his life to letting the sunshine into the lives of others by cleaning their windows.

"I want to make people happy," Wright said. "And a lot of people are happy when their windows are clean."

I knew I would be happy if my windows were clean because it also would give happiness to Sue, who had been after me for the past two years to use Windex and a roll of paper towels, not to mention a little elbow grease, to clean the windows.

"Elbow grease is a prime source of smudges and streaks," I told her.

Sue wasn't buying it, which is why I ended up buying a reasonably priced cleaning package (ten windows for $49) so she could finally meet Mr. Wright.

"I'm David," he said, introducing himself to Sue. "I'm here to clean your windows."

Sue swooned. "Thank you," she replied. "They could use it."

Wright started on the outside, where he told me that his wife, Joanne, likes the way he does the windows at their house but wishes he would do them more often.

"I'm working seven days a week," he said, adding that he started the business last year and will be joined next year by his son Collier, a U.S. Army Ranger who is serving in Iraq. "So I don't have the time to do our windows too often."

"That excuse isn't going to work for me," I said.

"You'll have to think of another one," Wright said as he used a water-fed pole with a nylon brush to clean the outside of the windows in the living, dining, and family rooms.

"Nylon?" I said. "Theoretically, I could clean windows with my wife's stockings."

"Theoretically," Wright responded, "it wouldn't be a good idea."

What would be a good idea, he added, is to use resin instead of soap. "I'm using it now," he said. "It's much more effective."

As he worked, Wright, who is fifty-three, told me that he started out as a lawyer ("If you go to the bathroom, bring work with you so you can bill your clients"), then got into financial services before giving up all his material possessions and spending time in a monastery, where he decided he wanted to make people happy for a living.

"I am doing my second-favorite thing," he said, referring to cleaning windows, which allows him to meditate while he works.

"What's your favorite thing?" I inquired.

"I'd like to be a professional poker player," Wright said. "But my wife doesn't think it's a safe bet."

When we moved inside, Wright said that customers always kid him about having the same name as the Mets star. "They'll say, 'When you finish with my windows, are you going to Citi Field?' Maybe I should give them my autograph," said Wright, who cleaned the windows with a long razor blade encased in a scraper. He also used a squeegee and a scrubber made of lamb's wool and AstroTurf.

"And I use Dawn," he said.

"Who's she?" I asked.

"The person you can get to clean your windows," said Wright, though he really meant the dishwashing liquid. "Don't tell your wife, but most windows are dirtier on the inside than they are on the outside."

I didn't tell Sue, who was nonetheless amazed when Wright was finished.

"Wow!" she squealed. "These windows have never been so clean."

"The trick," Wright said, "is to keep them that way."

"I'll do my part," I said. "In two years, I'll give you another call."

"This Guy Really Delivers"

With apologies to Nathaniel Hawthorne, who is dead and can't sue me, I live in the House of the Three Gables. When the vent in the main one, the Clark Gable, was gone with the wind after a recent storm, Sue asked me to fix it, to which I replied, "Frankly, my dear, I don't give a damn."

So we hired handyman extraordinaire Arnie Larsen, who happens to be our mailman. In addition to his day job at the U.S. Postal Service, Arnie is a carpenter who also does roofing, flooring, and all kinds of other work.

"I can pretty much build a house except for major plumbing and electrical," said Arnie, who has even worked on a clamming boat.

"You're a man of many hats," I said, "although it would probably be difficult to wear them all at the same time."

"Especially in the mail truck," said Arnie, adding that he enjoys his job as a letter carrier and has worked hard in the fourteen years he has been with the post office.

"Do the people on your route ask you to stop bringing them bills?" I wondered.

"All the time," he said. "They also want to know if it's cold enough for me or hot enough for me."

"So it's true that neither snow nor rain nor heat nor gloom of night stays you from the swift completion of your appointed rounds?" I asked.

"Yes," Arnie said. "Except if there's a blizzard like the one we got this year. It's tough to make it through three feet of snow."

"At least you didn't bring me any bills," I noted.

"Most people are very nice," Arnie said. "On really hot days, they'll bring me bottles of cold water. Or they'll leave one in the mailbox. Some of them tell me the neighborhood gossip, like who's having an affair and stuff like that. Then there are the women who shop online or order things from a catalog and don't want their husbands to know how much they bought, so they ask me to leave their packages next door. It doesn't matter because a lot of guys don't even open the mail."

"How about dogs?" I asked.

"They don't open the mail, either," Arnie said. "I like dogs, but I did get bitten once. I made friends with this cute Jack Russell terrier and petted him every day. One day he decided to see what I tasted like. It was only a nip, but I guess he didn't like the flavor because he left me alone after that. There was also this boxer that chased me. I had to hide in the bushes."

Arnie's adventures haven't been confined to his postal career.

"When I was a young man," recalled Arnie, who's forty-two, "I was on a home improvement job when the homeowner's wife came downstairs naked to do the laundry. I had to hide behind a wall. I sat on a spackle bucket until she went back upstairs. I told my boss and he laughed. The homeowner laughed, too. When it came time to collect my money, the boss said, 'You already got paid.'"

Another homeowner tried to help Arnie and fell through the ceiling.

"He came down in the kitchen," Arnie said.

"You won't get any help like that from me," I assured him. "I couldn't even fix the gable vent."

"I bet you could have," said Arnie, who climbed up to the roof and replaced the vent in no time. His work was so good and his fee was so reasonable that we may hire him to put a new floor in the living room.

"Don't worry about paying me right away," Arnie said. "I'll just leave a bill in the mailbox."

CHAPTER 4

"How to Babysit a Grandpa"

Being a grandfather comes with many important responsibilities, such as making funny faces, engaging in baby talk, and otherwise behaving like a child, which is pretty much how I acted even before I was a grandfather.

At the top of the list of grandfatherly duties is babysitting. But I never stopped to ask, because I am new at this, who is supposed to be babysitting whom?

I found out when I read "How to Babysit a Grandpa," a New York Times bestseller by children's author Jean Reagan.

The book, which features delightful illustrations by Lee Wildish, is for readers five to eight years old, right in the middle of my intellectual age group.

"It's also for readers in your physical age group," Reagan told me when I called her to talk about the thirty-two-page masterpiece. "After all, I couldn't leave out the grandpas."

"We appreciate it," I responded, "especially since we are the ones who have to be babysat."

Chloe, who's five months old, is a little too young to understand the lessons in the book (at the rate she's developing, that won't happen for another couple of weeks), but I feel better knowing that she will soon be able to look after me.

"She will love taking care of you because you sound like a lot of fun," said Reagan, who based the grandpa in the book on her father.

"My dad is a very funny guy who has always been attentive to my kids," Reagan said. "Of course, he did some things that I couldn't put in the book, like showing my son, who was then six or seven, how to make a slingshot. That means every grandpa whose grandchild read the book would be asked to make a slingshot. I can picture a lot of broken windows."

Speaking of which, the book opens with a clear view through the front window of the grandchild hiding when his grandpa rings the doorbell. After he greets his grandpa, and his parents drive away, the kid says, "When your mom and dad leave, pat your grandpa's hand and say, 'Don't worry. They always come back.' Then, right away, ask him if he's hungry."

"Snacks for Grandpa" are: "ice cream topped with cookies," "olives served on fingertips," "anything dipped in ketchup," and "cookies topped with ice cream."

"After snacks," the kid continues, "it's time to take your grandpa for a walk. ... Remember to grab his hand when you cross the street and remind him to look both ways."

Other parts include "What to Do on a Walk" ("If there's a puddle or a sprinkler, show him what to do"), "How to Entertain a Grandpa" ("Somersault across the room"), and "How to Play With a Grandpa" ("Give him a kazoo").

"When your grandpa says, 'Naptime,' it's time for his nap," the grandchild says. "The best way to put him to sleep is to have him read a loooooooong book, over and over and over and ... *zzzzzzz*."

After the grandpa wakes up, it's time to clean up the messes he has made. When the parents return, the kid says, "See, Grandpa. They always come back." Then he asks, "When can I babysit you again?"

"I wanted to be a little subversive and put a funny twist on things, but I also wanted to include lessons for kids," said Reagan. "Most of all, I wanted them to laugh."

The book is hilarious. And Reagan is working on another one that will be out next year.

"It's for grandmas," she said. "I'm not a grandma yet, but when I am, I want to be a fun one, like you're a fun grandpa."

"I'm sure my wife will love it," I said. "But for now, as my granddaughter will soon find out, she has her hands full babysitting me."

"Cool Customers"

If you can't stand the heat, get out of the family room. Or, even better, buy a new air conditioner.

That's what Sue and I did because the old air conditioner, which was in a wall sleeve in the family room when we moved into our house sixteen years ago, was beginning to spew out even more hot air than I do.

So we decided to play it cool and get one that actually works.

"Will you be installing it yourself?" asked a salesman at the appliance store.

"Not unless the warranty covers my hospital stay," I responded.

Thus did Kevin Beyer and his stepnephew, Matt Grescuk, arrive on a Saturday afternoon to remove the old air conditioner, an asthmatic hulk that looked like it belonged in a Model T, and install the new unit, a high-tech appliance that looks like it belongs on the Starship Enterprise and weighs about as much as a baby grand piano.

"I would have ruptured a vital organ doing this," I said.

"I just saved your life," replied Kevin, who told me, after he and Matt had ripped out the old air conditioner, that we had the wrong electrical outlet. "You need a 220 for the new air conditioner," he said, noting that we had a 110.

I called Sue on her cellphone to ask what we should do, as if either one of us could make the switch without getting electrocuted, but she didn't pick up, so I left a message. A few minutes later, she arrived home and said, "I was getting my nails done."

"That's another reason why I couldn't install the new air conditioner," I told Kevin. "I didn't want to break a nail."

"Most guys don't want to be bothered with stuff like this, so you're not alone," Kevin said. "Then there are the ones who think they're handy. They try to do things themselves and of course they mess up and their wives just roll their eyes. Most of the time, their wives are handier than they are."

"That's the case here," Sue chimed in.

"So you mean that ignorance really is bliss?" I said.

"For a lot of guys, yes," said Kevin. "For me, it's good for business."

"Are you handy?" I asked.

"I'm here, aren't I?" he said, adding that he owns KSB Construction in Commack, New York. "I install air conditioners on the side."

"That's appropriate," I said, "considering this one is on the side of the house."

Kevin nodded and continued, "I do roofing, kitchens, bathrooms, you name it."

"I'm petrified of heights," I said, "so I don't go on the roof."

"I can't get this body up there anymore," confessed Kevin, a burly man of forty-six. "I let my guys do it for me."

That includes Matt, who at nineteen is about the same age Kevin was when he got into this line of work. "I've learned a lot from him," Matt said. "Especially roofing," he added with a smile.

When we went outside so Kevin could make sure the new air conditioner was in the sleeve properly, Sue said she wanted to do some gardening, so she asked me to get her a trowel and a pair of gloves from the shed. I emerged with them a moment later.

"See, you're not totally useless after all," Kevin said, adding that he and Matt would take away our old air conditioner.

"If I left it on the curb, someone might steal it," I joked.

"Don't laugh," said Matt. "Someone would."

"Don't forget to call an electrician," Kevin advised. "Once you get the new AC up and running, your wife won't have to worry about your hot air anymore."

"Laundry Basket Case"

Life is a vicious cycle because there is always a laundry list of things to do. This is especially true if you have to do the laundry, in which case there are three cycles: wash, rinse, and spin.

But you can't do the laundry, as Sue and I found out recently, if your washing machine is on the fritz. Unfortunately, we don't know anybody named Fritz, so we called a plumber named Harry.

Harry, who owns Brookhaven Plumbing and Heating on Long Island, came over because our laundry room was beginning to flood.

The problem, we thought, was coming from the washer, a decrepit machine that had many clothes calls in its fifteen years (that's about a hundred in appliance years) but now seemed to be a victim of death by drowning.

Then we discovered a leak coming from the pipe under the slop sink, into which the washer regurgitated water, suds, and lint, which is not immaterial. In fact, I have a navel reserve of lint, but that's another story.

The real story, according to Harry, was that the elbow was leaking.

"Will I have to see a rheumatologist?" I asked.

"Not your elbow," Harry answered. "The sink's elbow. You need a plumbing doctor. That would be me."

"Thanks for making a house call, doc," I said.

"That's my job," said Harry, who noted that most insurance claims are the result of plumbing problems. "A washing machine hose will blow and cause a flood," he said. "I've gotten calls from people who had four feet of water in their basement."

"I'll never have that problem because I don't have a basement," I said.

"The water would just go through the garage," said Harry.

"Then my daughters would have to get all their stuff out of there," I said.

Harry's daughter has two daughters who are, of course, Harry's granddaughters.

"They're five and two years old," Harry said. "And they're always asking questions, like 'Papa, why is the sky blue?'"

"Do they ask plumbing questions?" I asked.

"I haven't gotten that yet," Harry answered. "But they know I can fix anything. They'll say to their mother, 'Mommy, call Papa. He knows how to do it.'"

"My granddaughter is only a year old," I said, "but I think she already knows that I can't fix anything."

Harry fixed the problem under the sink and attached a new hose from the washer to the slop sink, which he guessed was installed by the house's previous owner, a handy guy who had his own workshop in the garage.

"He probably came in here to wash his hands before he went into the kitchen so his wife wouldn't yell at him," surmised Harry, whose wife does the laundry in their house. "We have one of those high-tech machines with all these fancy features. It's just one more thing to go wrong. When we get another washer, it's going to be a simple one."

The next day, our washer conked out. Sue went to a nearby appliance store and bought a new, high-tech model that plays a tune when the wash is done.

The day after it was installed, I called Harry to tell him that he did an excellent job on the sink but that we ended up needing a new washer after all.

"You jinxed me," Harry said. "The day after I was at your house, our washer conked out, too. My wife got another high-tech model."

"Don't worry, Harry," I said. "It all comes out in the wash."

"Running Hot and Cold"

As a guy who is usually in hot water, which I am using as an excuse for all my wrinkles, I recently found myself in the unusual situation of being in hot water because there was no hot water.

Actually, there was hot water, but it left me cold because it was dripping out of the faucet in an upstairs bathroom. To prevent the American equivalent of Chinese water torture from keeping me awake at night and driving me even crazier than I already am, I had to open the vanity door and stick my empty head under the sink, an area so small that a Chihuahua would have felt claustrophobic, so I could turn off the hot water.

When I wanted to shave, I had to reverse the process. Then I reversed it again so the water bill wouldn't rival the gross national product of Finland.

This went on for months. Finally, at the strong suggestion of Sue, who doesn't even shave, I was faced with two choices: fix the problem or grow a beard.

Because I didn't want to look like Presidents Abraham Lincoln and James A. Garfield, both of whom were shot to death, I decided to go with Choice Number One.

This entailed disassembling the faucet so I could change the washer. Inasmuch as I am the least handy man in America, visions of Niagara Falls flooded my brain, which has water on it anyway.

I sought the wise counsel of Frank and Jerry, two ace maintenance guys at work.

"Make sure," Frank advised, "that you turn off the water or you'll have an indoor swimming pool."

"Maybe," Jerry added, "you should wear a bathing suit."

"How do I get the cap off the hot-water spigot?" I asked.

"Use a screwdriver," Frank answered.

"You mean vodka and orange juice?" I wondered.

"Whatever works," Jerry said.

I also talked with Gary, a talented colleague who used to write a home-improvement column. He printed out instructions with an illustration of the sink's parts, including the handle seat, the gasket, and, of course, the washer. The whole thing looked like the battle plans for the invasion of Normandy.

"There's a tool for taking the faucet apart," Gary said.

"Yes," I replied. "It's called a jackhammer. All I want to do is change the washer. Do I have to buy a new house?"

"Go on YouTube," Gary said, "and watch a video. It will show you how to do it."

So I did. The two-minute video, "How to Replace a Washer in a Leaky Faucet for Dummies," will never win an Oscar, but it was clearly aimed at me. And it was pretty instructive.

I used my smartphone, which has a dumb owner, to take a picture of the faucet. Then I went to Home Depot for further assistance.

I got it from Charlie, who is so knowledgeable that he coaches new recruits at the store. He assured me that I am not as incompetent as I think I am.

"My uncle was worse," Charlie said. "He was a brilliant lawyer who became a judge, but he couldn't change a light bulb. He eventually went blind, which didn't help."

Charlie informed me that my faucet doesn't have washers.

"You have to remove the nut," he said.

"That would be me," I countered.

"And," Charlie continued, "replace the cartridge."

"Do I have to use dynamite?" I asked.

"No," Charlie said. "A wrench will do. But turn off the water first."

"Even I know that," I said.

I bought a replacement cartridge, went home, turned off the water under the bathroom sink, and, much to my amazement (and Sue's), fixed the problem.

"Nice job," Sue said. "And we didn't even have to call a plumber."

Unfortunately, now something's wrong with the kitchen faucet. Looks like I'm in hot water again.

"The Appliance Whisperer"

Inanimate objects are out to get me. I can deal with human beings, either by ignoring them or by telling them such dumb jokes that they ignore me. But machines have me baffled.

That goes especially for the appliances in my house, which have conspired to drive me even crazier than I already am.

Fortunately, a fellow human, Leo Kasden, aka the Appliance Whisperer, has come to the rescue.

Leo, eighty-three, ace salesman at the P.C. Richard & Son store in Stony Brook, New York, sold both an air conditioner and a washing machine to me and Sue last year. Earlier this year, he sold us a dryer.

This was necessitated by the sad and expensive fact that all three of the old appliances conked out within months of each other. And recently, Sue and I have been the victims of more appliance mayhem.

In the span of about two weeks, we had trouble with the microwave, the toaster, and the coffee maker, none of which Leo sold us, though he did have some words of wisdom about these and all other appliances: "You have to talk to them," he said. "Maybe they're misbehaving because they think you don't like them."

Leo loves appliances. He has been selling them for sixty years, the past forty at P.C. Richard, an East Coast chain founded in 1909.

"I can't wait to come to work every day," Leo told me.

"Aren't you going to retire?" I asked.

"I'll retire when the Jets win the Super Bowl," Leo said of his favorite football team.

"You may be working forever," I remarked.

Leo nodded and said, "That's OK. I love my job. It's challenging because you have to be like a doctor and keep up with the latest technology. When I started, there were ice boxes and black-and-white TVs. Now you have washers and dryers that look like they came out of 'Star Trek.' The ones you and your wife bought are like that."

"They even play a little tune when the wash is done," I said. "It was catchy at first, but now I can't get that stupid song out of my head. I'm sure it's part of the appliance conspiracy against me."

"It's like in the James Patterson book 'Zoo,' with the rebellion of the animals," Leo said. "This could be the rebellion of the appliances."

"I wouldn't be surprised," I said, telling Leo about the mind games the microwave played on me. "I was making popcorn when the fan went on and wouldn't go off. We had to call in a technician, who was totally baffled. The day after he left, the fan went off and the microwave started working again."

Then there was the toaster.

"We had a brand-new one and it just stopped working," I recalled. "Maybe it's because I put in a slice of bread and pressed the 'bagel' button, just to be cute. I mean, how would it know?"

"They know when you try to fool them," said Leo.

"And the coffee maker was so bad that the coffee was lukewarm," I said. "We had to heat it up in the microwave. When the fan was on, we couldn't have coffee at all."

"Not a good way to start the day," said Leo, adding that his wife, Harriet, to whom he has been married for as long as he has been in sales, operates all the appliances at home. "She cooks and does the laundry. I leave the machines alone."

"Maybe I should do the same thing," I said. "I used to do the laundry, but my wife won't let me now that we have a new washer and dryer. She's afraid I'll break them."

"If you check out your appliances every morning and say hello to them, that might help," Leo suggested. "Maybe they'll like you better."

"Dishes Your Life"

I'm the very model of the modern mixed-up man. And I have long been baffled by one of the great mysteries of domestic life: If a dishwasher washes dishes, why do you have to wash the dishes before putting them in the dishwasher?

That is the question I have been asking Sue for the past thirty-seven years.

Her thoroughly convincing answer: "Because."

It does no good to point out that in television commercials for dishwashers, or even for dishwashing detergent, dishes that are encrusted with food chunks the consistency of concrete always come out shiny and spotless.

That wasn't the case in our house. In a spiteful act that would never be shown on TV, the dishwasher conked out. So I had to wash the dishes by hand.

Sometimes Sue washed them and I dried. Or I left them in the dish drainer to dry, which prompted Sue to ask, "Why aren't you drying the dishes?"

My thoroughly unconvincing answer: "Because."

One thing was clear (and it wasn't the wine glass I streaked with a damp dish towel): You don't appreciate something until you don't have it anymore.

That's the way Sue and I felt about the dishwasher, which had served us well for about a dozen years before dying of what I can only assume was food poisoning.

This forced us to wash dishes the old-fashioned way. When doing so, you have to place a basin in the kitchen sink and fill it with water hot enough to scald the hide off a crocodile. First, however, you should squirt in a stream of dishwashing liquid, which will make enough bubbles to obscure the utensils and cause you to slice your thumb on a steak knife.

To prevent me from bleeding to death, which would have stained the counters, Sue bought — and forgive me for being too technical here — a dishwashing thingie. It has a long handle with a screw top on one end, so you can put in detergent, and a brush on the other, so you can scrub the dishes.

That way you don't have to fill a basin. Instead, you can let the water run for such a long time that it would overflow Lake Superior, which isn't a good place to wash dishes anyway.

But you have to get them clean because you need something to eat on. After a while, however, taking nourishment intravenously seems like an appealing alternative.

The situation, like the water, reached a boiling point. This happened after dinner one night when I seriously considered killing one of the actors in a dishwasher commercial and going to prison so I wouldn't have to wash the dishes anymore. But then, I figured, I'd be assigned kitchen duty for the rest of my life.

Before I could say to Sue, "We really ought to buy a new dishwasher," Sue said to me, "We really ought to buy a new dishwasher."

So she went to an appliance store and bought one. But when it was delivered, it didn't fit because the measurements were wrong. (The dishwasher's, not Sue's.)

Back to the store went Sue. And back to our house went another dishwasher.

The delivery guys, Tom and Anthony, sympathized with our plight.

"You don't want to be without a dishwasher for too long," Tom said.

"It's bad when you have to wash the dishes yourself," Anthony chimed in.

After much measuring, and maneuvering, and manpower, Tom and Anthony got the dishwasher to fit.

Then came the moment of truth: "I'm going to give it a test run," Tom said.

Sue and I held our breath, collectively thinking, "Please, God, make it work. And don't flood the kitchen."

Tom pressed some buttons.

"It's so quiet," Sue noted.

"Unlike me," I added.

The dishwasher ran, the water drained, and, lo, there was no flood in the kitchen.

That evening, with spotless wine glasses, Sue and I toasted our new dishwasher.

"I'll load it," I said after dinner.

"Thanks," Sue said. "And don't forget to wash the dishes before you put them in."

CHAPTER 5

"Princely Postcard"

It would not be classic British understatement to say that Prince Charles and I have a lot in common.

For one thing, as Sue would attest, we both spend an inordinate amount of time on the throne.

For another, Charles and I are first-time grandfathers.

And now, it seems, we are pen pals.

That is why I was not surprised to receive a reply to the missive I sent to Charles earlier this year to congratulate him on being a new grandpa.

I said, in part, that our families have some amazing similarities, including the fact that his older son, William, and daughter-in-law, Kate, were married in England the day before Lauren and Guillaume were married in France in 2011. And that Chloe and Charles's grandson, George, while not born on the same day, each arrived at exactly 4:24 p.m., which means they are likely destined for each other. I even envisioned a royal wedding. I closed by saying that Charles will enjoy being a grandfather as much as I do and that we should set up a play date for the kids.

Imagine my delight when I received an envelope by royal mail with a return address of Buckingham Palace.

I opened it to find a postcard with a photo of Charles and his lovely wife, Camilla. The caption read: "The Prince of Wales and The Duchess of Cornwall leaving St. Mary's Hospital after meeting Prince George for the first time."

The message, in serif italic typeface, read:

"The Prince of Wales was most touched that you took the trouble to write as you did on the birth of His Royal Highness's first grandchild, Prince George.

"His Royal Highness appreciated your kind words and sends you his warmest thanks and best wishes."

Frankly, I was a little disappointed. Since Charles and I are so close, I expected a handwritten note, or at least a personalized response, like the letter I received after I wrote to William and Kate to congratulate them on their wedding. The reply was written by Mrs. Claudia Holloway, head of correspondence for the royal family. She opened with "Dear Mr. Zezima," and wrote, in part, "The Duke and Duchess of Cambridge have asked me to send you their warmest thanks together with their belated congratulations to Lauren and Guillaume." She signed the letter with a distinctive flourish in royal blue ink.

I was, to use Prince Charles's words, most touched.

Not this time. I was, to put it mildly, most peeved.

But then I realized that the Prince of Wales must be too busy being a grandfather to send out handwritten notes or personalized responses.

If Charles is like me, he has been doing a lot of babysitting. This would entail holding George on his knee while watching sports (polo or cricket matches or maybe even soccer games) on TV. It would also entail the grand British tradition of doing your duty for God, country, and, yes, baby. As I am sure Charles has found out, the changing of the guard takes on a whole new meaning when you're a grandfather.

Then there are projects such as the one I undertook the other night. I may be the least handy man in America (I don't imagine Charles is Mr. Fixit across the pond), but I did manage to put together a highchair without incident or bloodshed. I would advise Charles to follow the instructions carefully and not use language that would be considered a departure from the King's English.

So, no, I am not miffed at the Prince of Wales. In fact, I understand his time constraints completely. Still, if he wants more advice on how to be a good grandfather, all he has to do is write me a letter.

"The Polo Pony Whisperer"

A horse is a horse, of course, of course, and no one can talk to a horse, of course — unless, of course, you're a newspaper columnist who gets an exclusive interview with a champion polo pony.

That's what I did recently when I hoofed it out to Riverhead, New York, for the Sandy Relief Charity Polo Match at the Dorothy P. Flint

Camp. The match drew about four hundred people and raised more than $10,000 for the 4-H program at the camp, which is run by the Cornell Cooperative Extension of Nassau County.

The first thing I noticed was that Prince Harry wasn't there. Harry recently played in a charity polo match in Greenwich, Connecticut, but was conspicuously absent from the Long Island event.

"He's missing a good time," said Nick Aliano, owner of Aliano Real Estate, which sponsored the match.

The sport of kings would have liked to have the prince, but it got several of the next best things in players who are rated as high or higher than Harry by the United States Polo Association.

That includes Aliano, fifty-seven, who took up the sport thirteen years ago and is rated at one goal. Ratings go from minus-two to ten, with ninety-seven percent of players being rated at zero goals or fewer.

"You're as good as Harry," I said after finding out that the prince also is rated at one goal.

"I guess that makes me a prince of a guy," said Aliano, who showed me some of his horses, all Thoroughbreds that are the real athletes in the sport.

"Ninety percent of the game is the horse," said Alberto Bengolea, a player and trainer who has a reputation as a horse whisperer.

"I whisper, but the horses don't listen," said Bengolea, sixty-one, who has worked with the animals for most of his life.

When I introduced myself to Catherine, one of Aliano's horses, she looked at me and sighed. Then she looked away.

"She's saying, 'I don't care about you. Let's just get this over with.' Right now, she's napping," Bengolea told me.

"I put her to sleep?" I said. "I have that effect on people. I had no idea I could do it to horses, too."

Fortunately, the other horses I spoke with (or whispered to) didn't doze off. But I had to wait until halftime of the match, a spirited affair between Aliano Real Estate and the 4-H Crusaders.

At the intermission, I had the honor of interviewing Pinton, on whom Aliano was riding when he scored a goal to help give his team a 4-1 lead.

"He scored the goal," Aliano said of Pinton, who actually nodded when I asked him if it felt good to help his club.

"He's a team player," said Aliano, who allowed me to mount a horse named Sixty-nine, a gentle veteran that graciously stood still while Bengolea handed me a polo mallet. He showed me the proper way to hold it and how to swing it should I ever find myself playing in a polo match, in which case I would surely be rated minus-two.

"Or maybe I'd be off the charts," I suggested.

Sixty-nine nodded, too.

The second half was even more exciting than the first, as the Crusaders rallied to tie the match, 7-7. But Aliano, who had three goals and was named best player, scored the decisive tally in a 9-7 victory.

As his team was awarded the Cornell Cup, the players sprayed each other with Champagne, some of which got on Pistola, who was named best playing pony.

"She doesn't drink Champagne, but she likes the spray," said her owner, Lobo Fernandez, thirty-five, who scored three goals atop the twelve-year-old gray speckled champion. "She's a really great horse."

"Congratulations, champ," I said to Pistola. "How does it feel?"

Pistola looked at me and lowered her head in modesty.

"She doesn't like to brag," Fernandez said. "But she feels good. She had a terrific match."

And it was all for a good cause. Too bad Prince Harry missed it.

"Three Chairs for Jerry"

A man's home is his hassle. That's why he needs a throne to sit on. And I'm not talking about one made of porcelain.

I refer, of course, to a guy chair — a big, comfortable seat he can relax in after performing such exhausting tasks as throwing out the garbage or picking up his dirty socks and underwear, a place fit for a king while he sits in front of the TV and either watches sports for hours on end or struggles to stay awake for the eleven o'clock news.

Sue, bless her heart, said I needed one. So we went furniture shopping.

When we arrived at the store, Sue told the greeter, who did her job well by greeting us, that we had an appointment with a saleswoman named Melody. The greeter telephoned Melody, who was in another part of the store, and said, "There are guests at the front desk."

"This sounds like a hotel," I said. "If we're guests, can we stay overnight?"

"Sure," the greeter answered. "We have bedroom furniture upstairs."

I noticed a bar with wine glasses and empty bottles.

"Did I miss happy hour?" I asked.

"Yes," the greeter said. "We just finished the wine."

While we were waiting for Melody, I walked around the store, which probably had more chairs, tables, beds, bureaus, sofas, and nightstands than Buckingham Palace. There were enough footstools for an ottoman empire.

"Try out the chairs," Sue suggested.

"You want me to sit around and do nothing?" I asked. "That's what I do at home."

At that point, Melody showed up and said she was helping another customer but that we would be in good hands with Gloria.

"We're looking for a chair," Sue told her.

"What kind?" Gloria inquired.

"A guy chair," I said. "For me."

Then I proceeded to tell Gloria the long, sad story of the history of all the chairs that were supposed to be for me but were co-opted by Sue or our various pets, including our late, beloved dog, Lizzie, and our still-living cats, Kitty and her fat daughter, Bernice.

"The first time we got a chair that was ostensibly for me, we put it in the family room and Sue started sitting in it to watch 'Law & Order' and all her other shows," I explained. "I was relegated to the rocking chair. At least I got to practice for my old age, which is rapidly approaching."

"You don't look old," said Gloria.

"That's because I'm shockingly immature," I replied. "It makes me seem younger."

Sue agreed.

"Anyway," I continued, "the chair was getting clawed by our cats, so Sue put a slipcover on it. Then she said we needed another chair."

"It was supposed to be for him," Sue chimed in.

"Was it?" Gloria asked.

"No," I said. "Sue started using it and our dog took over the first chair. She didn't even watch 'Law & Order.' We put it in the living room, which we seldom use. I still sat in the rocking chair."

"Now we're looking for a third chair," Sue said. "This time it's really for Jerry."

I picked out a very comfortable club chair that matched the sofa and the second chair.

"It's the only chair that Cindy Crawford attaches herself to," Gloria informed me. "She uses it for her collection."

"Does this mean Cindy will be visiting us to watch TV?" I asked excitedly.

"She doesn't come with the chair," Gloria responded.

"That's OK," I said. "She'd only take it over and I'd have to sit in the rocker again."

The new club chair was delivered a few days later and put in the family room. I'd like to say I enjoy it, but our cats have taken it over.

As always, I am not going to take this sitting down.

CHAPTER 6

"A Twin-Win Situation"

In the year since Chloe was born, I have said she is twice as beautiful as any other baby in the world.

It turns out I am right. That's because it took two babies to win the Gerber Photo Search, a nationwide contest sponsored by the infant and toddler food company. The latest competition, the fourth annual, drew 156,000 entries, including Chloe.

The winners are Levi and Paxton Strickland, one-year-old identical twin brothers from Wernersville, Pennsylvania, who are, I must admit, adorable.

In a press release, Bernadette Tortorella, integrated marketing manager at Gerber, said, "There were so many entries that fit our criteria, but the judges were in awe of the Strickland twins," adding: "Every baby is a Gerber baby."

That includes Chloe, who likes to snack on Gerber Graduates Apple-Cinnamon Puffs.

But in the spirit of good sportsmanship, I called Levi and Paxton to congratulate them on winning the contest, which comes with a grand prize of $50,000 and the chance to appear in a Gerber advertisement.

The twins must have been busy playing, which is, at this point, their job, because their mother, Amanda, answered the phone.

"Winning the contest is very exciting," Amanda said, "but the boys haven't let it go to their heads."

I found that out when I asked Amanda to put the phone to those two handsome heads, which are topped with light hair and dominated by big blue eyes and wide smiles.

"Here's Levi," said Amanda.

"Congratulations, Levi!" I said. "You're a star."

Levi was too modest to reply, but he must have been doing something funny because I heard giggles in the background.

"Paxton's laughing," Amanda explained. "He's the laid-back one. Levi is our little jokester. He's always making his brother crack up."

"My granddaughter, Chloe, loves to laugh, too," I said. "She has a great sense of humor. And she's really smart. She gets that from her mommy and daddy, not from me."

"I bet the boys would like to meet her," Amanda replied.

"Maybe we could set up a play date," I said, adding that with the twins and her husband, Matt, Amanda is surrounded by guys. "It's the opposite with me," I noted. "My wife and I have two daughters and now there's Chloe, so I'm surrounded by women."

"The boys love their daddy," Amanda said. "But I'm with them during the day and we have fun."

Amanda, twenty-four, has started a home-based business selling essential oils; Matt, twenty-six, is the production manager for a technology company.

Amanda and I compared notes on the kids. Levi and Paxton, who were born on Matt's birthday, are about a month older than Chloe, but all three are babbling ("I do that, too," I admitted) and are about to take their first steps.

"Time for the grown-ups to buy track shoes," I said, adding that the prize money could pay for a lot of them.

"That's going into the boys' college fund," said Amanda.

"Save some of it to buy them track shoes, too," I said. "It could lead to college scholarships. The prize money is nice, but it won't cover everything."

As for being in a Gerber ad or doing personal appearances, nothing as been set up yet, said Amanda, adding: "The boys would like it."

"If they can't make it to an appearance, Chloe could fill in," I suggested.

"I'm sure she would be great," said Amanda.

"Congratulations again to Levi and Paxton," I said.

"The twins appreciate your call," Amanda said. "And they send their love to Chloe."

"It's About Crime"

When I was a kid, I wanted to be a private eye (my other eye, I figured, would be public), but I never pursued it because I was sure I'd end up investigating myself.

Now that I am an adult who does not (as yet) have a criminal record, I thought it would finally be a good time to take a class on how to be a detective.

So I signed up at the Center Moriches Library on Long Island for "Junior Crime Investigators," a four-session course that teaches kids how to investigate crimes like those seen on the TV show "CSI."

The instructor was Larissa Froeschl, a forensic science teacher who has worked with law-enforcement officials and has a master's degree in biology.

The class was composed of about ten kids, all of whom were twelve, and one geezer, who was almost five times as old but only half as mature.

The first session, which like the others lasted an hour and a half, was a fingerprinting workshop.

"Your prints are hard to read," Larissa told me as she looked at them on my personal identification sheet. "Maybe you would be a good criminal."

Then, while wearing rubber gloves, the kids and I used ostrich-feather brushes and nontoxic powders to dust for fingerprints we put on items such as a glass tube, a soap dish, a butter knife, a hair clip, and, the one I used, a fake jewel.

"I could bring it home to my wife and tell her it's real," I said to Larissa.

"I can see your thumb print on it," she replied as she inspected the item with a magnifying glass. "Even though your fingerprints aren't too distinct, with modern forensics, you'd get caught."

"There goes my criminal career," I lamented.

I went from crook to kidnapping victim in the next class, which focused on ransom notes.

"You have to give handwriting samples," said Larissa, who instructed each of us to write the following sentence three times on a sheet of paper: "The quick brown fox jumps over the lazy dog."

Then she divided the class into two groups. A member of each group had to write a ransom note for the other group to solve. The note our group had to solve read: "We have your mustache! Give us two million dollars or we will sell it on eBay."

"It looks like you've been kidnapped," Larissa said.

"Who would want me?" I responded.

Possibly the cops, as I found out in the third session, for which Larissa had created a crime scene that was cordoned off with yellow police tape. Scattered over the floor were pieces of evidence, including a purse, a key, and a knife with ketchup on it.

"It could be the murder weapon," Larissa said.

"Or maybe somebody was making a sandwich with it," a student named Jack theorized.

After we all gave hair samples and looked at them under microscopes, Larissa said to me, "You have a nice medulla. Your hair has a very distinctive structure."

"I thought only my hairdresser knew for sure," I replied.

I escaped the hairy situation (Larissa was the guilty party), but I was a suspect in a jewel heist in the final class.

Actually, I was two suspects because I played dual roles: the husband of the princess whose jewels were stolen and a long-lost friend of hers. Larissa played the princess, her maid, and her secretary.

The kids had to use the skills they learned in the previous three classes to deduce the identity of the thief. They correctly collared the secretary.

"At least I'm not going to jail," I told Larissa at the end of the class.

"No," she said. "But maybe you can be a detective and get your own show."

I can see it now: "CSI: Column Stupidity Investigation."

"A Very Social Security Guard"

If the safety of other people depended upon me, a pretty frightening thought since I can't even protect myself, I would be an insecurity guard, stationed at the front desk of a building that anybody could enter but nobody would want to because, of course, I'd be guarding the place.

That is not the case with Herbert "Doc" Koenig, a security guard in the building where I work. He don't need no stinking badge (he has an ID card with a photo of his goateed visage and the word "Doc" under it) and he doesn't carry a pistol, mainly because he is one. But he does have a rapier wit that could disarm the most suspicious intruder.

That, on most days, would be me.

"I'm not a real doctor," Doc confessed during a midday break, "but I used to be an EMT in New York City and I delivered two of my kids, so people began calling me Doc."

Then he began recalling some of his EMT adventures. The most memorable was the time he had to rescue an obese woman who got stuck in a bathtub.

"This lady was quite large," Doc said. "The tub was drained and she couldn't budge. There was this sucking sound as we pulled her out. I tried not to laugh. She was embarrassed, but she had a good sense of humor. She said, 'At least I'm clean.'"

Then there was the time a young woman took her pants off on a busy Brooklyn street.

"She got hit by a car and her tibia was shattered," Doc recalled, "so we put her on a stretcher. She was wearing designer jeans. I was going to cut them off, which was protocol. She said, 'You're not going to cut these. They're Jordache jeans.' She hopped up on one leg in the middle of Flatbush Avenue and took her pants off. She said, 'I can wash out the blood, but I can't sew my jeans back up.'"

The people who didn't have a leg to stand on were some of the knuckleheads Doc met in New York Supreme Court in Manhattan, where he worked for thirty years, twenty-three as an arraignment sergeant.

"It's the busiest criminal court in the world," Doc said, "so you see some pretty crazy things."

Like the drug defendant who showed up in a T-shirt emblazoned with the words "Wacky Weedies" and a picture of a stoner smoking a blunt, which is a cigar filled with marijuana.

"You can't fix stupid," Doc noted.

Judges didn't always show good judgment, either.

"One of them berated a defendant," Doc remembered. "The guy didn't like what the judge said, so he threw a punch. The judge said, 'Aren't you going to protect me?' I said, 'If he hits you, it's assault, right?' Another time, a pro basketball player didn't like what a judge said. A fight broke out and I ended up with a size seventeen footprint on my leg."

But for Doc's money, the topper was the billionaire he was hired to protect.

"He was rich and nasty," Doc said. "And he was working on his fourth wife. I can't tell you who he is, but he's a real piece of work. If I had his money, I'd be rich but not nasty."

At fifty-six, he'd also be retired, spending time with his wife, four children, and two grandchildren.

"When the kids were growing up, I was the cool dad," Doc said. "All their friends would come over because we always had a lot of fun at our house. We still do. Now I'm the cool granddad, too."

Since Doc isn't a billionaire, he's working as a security guard, one of the friendly, dedicated people who protect the building where I work.

"You have to be nice," Doc said when I asked what it takes to do his job, "but you also have to be vigilant. And you have to watch out for suspicious characters."

"Like me?" I wondered.

"Sometimes," Doc said, "I'll let anybody in."

CHAPTER 7

"Grandfather's Security System"

When Katie and Lauren were just starting to toddle — a means of locomotion that, in my case, has often involved beer — Sue and I had to install latches and locks on the drawers and doors of our kitchen cabinets so the girls couldn't open them and spill the contents all over the floor.

It worked, at least in part, because it kept me out. To this day, I don't know where anything is.

Now that Chloe is crawling around at record speed and has taken her first tentative steps, we have to repeat the process when she comes over to visit.

I went to Babies R Us to buy childproofing equipment and got a refresher course from two very nice sales associates named Nikki and Jessica.

"A lot of the questions we get are about diapers and breast pumps," said Nikki.

"I don't think a breast pump would work on me, although I do like to milk a joke," I said. "As for diapers, I'm a geezer, so I guess it Depends."

"Most of our customers are moms," Jessica explained.

"How about dads?" I wondered.

"They come in once in a while," Jessica said. "They'll have a list of things their wives want them to get."

"The mom is either still in the hospital or has just gotten home after giving birth," Nikki noted. "She'll send the dad here to buy stuff. We pay special attention to him, especially if he's a new dad, because he's usually confused."

"How about grandfathers?" I asked.

"We don't get too many grandpas," Jessica said. "But when we do, they're usually confused, too."

"I'm a grandpa and I'm confused," I said.

"We can help you," said Nikki.

"Good," I said. "I'm looking for latches and locks so my granddaughter can't open the drawers and doors of our kitchen cabinets."

"How old is she?" Jessica asked.

"She's one," I responded.

"That's an active age," said Nikki. "They get into everything."

"Unfortunately," Jessica added, "many of the guys who come in for latches and locks aren't too handy. One guy wanted a lock that didn't have screws because it would be too much trouble to install."

"He probably didn't even have a screwdriver," Nikki said.

"All he would need," I suggested, "is vodka and orange juice."

"That would help," said Jessica.

"Or maybe not," Nikki added.

Nikki and Jessica showed me the store's childproofing equipment. It included a pack of twelve cabinet and drawer latches, which come with screws, and a pack of three cabinet slide locks, which don't.

"The slide locks fit on doorknobs and handles," Jessica said. "The latches are best for drawers. You have to screw them into the cabinet frames and the inside of the drawers."

"I'll take both packs," I said, thanking Nikki and Jessica for their help and insight.

The next day, I slid the slide locks through the door handles of three of our kitchen cabinets. It took about ten seconds, not bad considering it took about ten minutes to open the pack.

An hour later, Chloe came over. She scooted around, crawling even faster in the week since I last saw her and taking more tentative steps. She went into the kitchen and tried to open the cabinet doors, behind which are pots, pans, bowls, and other things that might have been spilled all over the floor.

Chloe tugged, but the locks worked, so she scooted off to play in the family room.

"Nice job," Sue told me. "Next you have to secure the drawers."

"No problem," I said. "The latches have screws. All I need is some vodka and orange juice."

"Car Talk"

In the four decades since I took a driver's ed class, I have become such a proficient motorist that I could teach a class myself except that I have two speeding tickets on my record and my name isn't Ed.

Still, in an effort to become less of a menace to society and, in the process, reduce my insurance rates, I recently took a refresher course from a guy who not only was named New York State Driving Instructor of the Year by the National Safety Council but has only one speeding ticket on his record.

"I was driving my son to college and I guess I was going a little too fast on the highway because I got pulled over," Marty Hirschfield explained. "My son was laughing at me in the backseat."

In fact, Hirschfield isn't even the best driver in his family.

"My wife is better than I am," he said.

"I could be in NASCAR," I told Hirschfield before the first of the two three-hour defensive-driving sessions, "but my SUV, which has 183,000 miles on it, can't do two hundred miles per hour."

"Then it's a good thing you're taking this class," he replied.

Hirschfield, who has worked for Driver Education Consultants for seventeen years, told me and my twenty-five classmates that we had to remember four important things: "One, if I ask you a question, humor me. Two, stay awake. Three, pay attention. Four, I need you to laugh at my bad jokes. And they're pretty bad."

Example: "In one class, I asked people to fill out the form all of you got. Where it said 'sex,' one woman wrote, 'Sometimes.' I said, 'Lady, that's more information than I wanted to know.'"

Hirschfield said that a lot of people take his course every three years but that very few of them remember what he said.

"I can tell the same jokes I told three years ago," he proclaimed. "I don't have to write new material."

Much of Hirschfield's material, which I was hearing for the first time, was pretty serious, such as the dangers of excessive speed, drinking and driving, texting and driving, and talking on a cellphone while driving.

"Nobody talks on a cellphone while they're watching their favorite TV show," Hirschfield said. "They don't want to be distracted. So why do they talk on the phone while they're driving?"

Good question. He asked plenty of others, as when he said to me, "Jerry, in the real world, what does a yellow light mean?"

My response: "Floor it!"

The class laughed knowingly. Hirschfield smiled and said, "That's right. Pedal to the metal. But what is it supposed to mean?"

"Caution," I replied.

Hirschfield said, "That's right. Slow down."

It was basic stuff that most people either forget or flout. But Hirschfield told us something that all but one person in the class didn't know.

"Can you ever make a left turn on red?" he asked.

Dorothy raised her hand and responded, "Yes, if you are coming out of a one-way street and turning onto another one-way street."

Hirschfield exclaimed, "That's right! You took my class three years ago. You must remember my bad jokes."

The scariest part, aside from the ten short films we saw, involved the penalties for drunken driving in other countries. In Malaysia, for example, a DWI offender is jailed, and if he is married, his wife is jailed, too.

"If that doesn't get you to stop drinking and driving," Hirschfield said, "nothing will."

All in all, the class was terrific, and our witty and insightful instructor was, of course, the driving force behind it. I even have a certificate to show I graduated.

"Drive home safely," Hirschfield told me on the way out. "After all, you don't want to get a speeding ticket."

"Wrong Turn on Red"

In their chart-topping 1965 hit, "Turn! Turn! Turn!," the Byrds sang, "To everything, turn, turn, turn." To which they might have added: "Except if you make an illegal turn, turn, turn." In which case you'll end up in traffic court.

That's where I found myself after getting a notice in the mail saying that I had been caught by a red-light camera making an illegal right turn at a traffic light.

Accompanying the notice was a series of three photos I was sure would vindicate me because they showed not only that it was perfectly legal to turn right on red, but that my brake lights were on at the intersection. Since the fine was $80, I decided to fight the charge because I had an otherwise clean driving record. This involved paying strict attention to traffic laws, being respectful of other drivers, and, most important, not getting caught rolling through right turns at red lights.

I showed up at the Nassau County Traffic and Parking Violations Agency in Hempstead, New York, and beheld scores of other alleged scofflaws who sought justice because they were, according to the U.S. Constitution and TV shows like "Law & Order," innocent until proven guilty of running stop signs, speeding, and, of course, making illegal right turns.

I temporarily surrendered my driver's license to a stern security officer and stood in line, where I met a woman named Surbi, who was there because, she said, "I parked in front of my house."

"Did you get a ticket the day you moved in?" I asked.

"No," she replied. "I've lived there for six years."

"I hope you don't have to pay six years' worth of parking tickets," I said.

"I couldn't afford it," Surbi said. "This one alone is $120. And there's not even a 'no parking' sign on the street."

After we were ushered into the courtroom, I sat next to a young woman named Linda, who admitted that she "rolled" through a stop sign. "I was being tailgated and didn't want the guy to plow into the back of my car," she explained.

"Tell it to the judge," I suggested.

"I will," Linda promised.

I showed her the photos of my car at the intersection. "This is Exhibit A," I said.

"They'll get you anyway," said a young guy named Jacques, adding that he had six tickets totaling $1,700 but that he could prove he was a victim of identity theft and that the car wasn't his.

Among the other people in the courtroom was a young man who was holding a toddler. An old lawyer said to him, "Did you rent that kid to get sympathy?"

Just then, my name was called by a court clerk named Laura, who took me to a hallway, sat me at a table with a computer screen, and pulled a shocker: "We have a video of you at the intersection," she said. It showed me braking but not coming to a "full and complete stop." Laura said I could pay the fine or see a judge, who would either uphold the fine or dismiss the charge.

"I know my rights," I said, though I guess I didn't because I had evidently made an illegal right. "I'll see a judge."

She was the Hon. Elizabeth Pessala, who was indeed honorable but went by the letter of the law when a smug traffic prosecutor showed her the video.

"It's a good thing you weren't stopped by a police officer," Judge Pessala said. "The fine would have been $218 and three points off your license."

"Guilty as charged, your honor," I confessed.

I paid the fine and drove home very carefully. After all, I didn't want one bad turn to deserve another.

"Miles to Go Before It Sleeps"

Any motorist knows that the best way to ensure longevity is to regularly check your parts, monitor your fluids, and make sure your undercarriage is clean.

You should do the same for your car.

That's why I am happy but not surprised that my sport utility vehicle recently hit 200,000 miles. Full credit for the fact that it is still running smoothly, which is more than I can say for myself most days, goes to Mary Husson, service manager at Hyundai 112 in Medford, New York.

"Oil is the lifeblood of the car," Mary said when I brought mine in for an oil change.

"You mean extra virgin olive oil?" I wondered.

"That could be the lifeblood of you," said Mary, who has been my car's primary care physician since I bought it in 2004. "It's also important to rotate your tires," she added.

"Don't I do that every time I drive?" I asked.

"Now I know why you don't work here," said Mary, who has three cars: a 2013 Hyundai Sonata, a 2011 Hyundai Elantra, and, her pride and joy, a 1999 Ford Mustang convertible that has only 63,000 miles on it.

"I keep the Mustang in the garage for six months," Mary said. "When the weather gets nice, I drive it with the top down."

"Can't you get arrested for doing that?" I inquired.

"Yes," Mary replied. "But at least I don't waste gas by using the air-conditioning."

Then Mary showed me cellphone photos of her adorable little granddaughter, Sophia, who's one. Not to be outdone, I showed Mary cellphone photos of Chloe, who's the same age.

"Chloe has her own little car at home," I said. "She loves when I push her around the house in it. Now that the weather's nice, we go outside."

"Does the car have 200,000 miles on it?" Mary asked.

"No," I said. "But sometimes it feels like my feet do."

"Going over 200,000 miles is not really a big deal," said Mary. "If you take good care of your vehicle, there's no reason why it shouldn't last longer. I knew a guy whose car had 275,000 miles on it. You could even hit 300,000."

Technician Anthony Busone agreed.

"It looks like you take pretty good care of it," he said as we stood under the vehicle, which was on a lift in the garage. "Some people don't."

Like the guy who never changed the brakes on his car.

"He got all the way down to the metal backings," Anthony recalled. "The rotors were worn away. He heard this thumping noise but didn't do anything about it. Miraculously, the car still stopped. I don't know what he would have said if it didn't."

"Those are the brakes," I offered.

Anthony, twenty-two, who has been a technician for three years, has a 1992 Honda Civic with 243,000 miles on it.

"You must change the oil regularly," I said.

"Yes," Anthony replied. "I've also changed the motor. Most people can't do that."

"I'd have an easier time transcribing the Dead Sea Scrolls than telling you what's under the hood of my car," I noted.

"You don't have to," said Anthony. "That's my job."

And he does it well. Fortunately, my car, a Hyundai Santa Fe, didn't need open-hood surgery.

"You do need a new air filter," Anthony said. "And your rear brakes are getting low. Don't be like that guy. We'll change them next time you're in. Other than that, it looks pretty good."

On the way out, I thanked Mary and said I'd see her in 3,000 miles for another oil change.

"Fluids are important," she emphasized.

"I know," I said. "Especially when you have the kind of mileage I do."

"If you want to keep going," Mary said, "drink a lot of Gatorade."

"All Pumped Up"

I am not much of a couch potato, not only because Sue won't let me eat potatoes on the couch while watching TV, but because I prefer to drink beer in the lounge chair.

But I am definitely a pump potato. That's because I am hooked on a channel called Gas Station TV.

I discovered it when I went to the gas station and was transfixed by the TVs in the new pumps.

"If I could fit my lounge chair in the car, I'd drive it over here so I could sit in Lane One and watch TV all day," I told Bree, the nice young man at the register.

"There's only one channel," he said, "but there's a lot on it."

"I know," I replied. "I just watched the weather forecast — it's supposed to rain — and I saw a car commercial, which was appropriate. The last time I was here, I watched the entertainment news and the sports update. A guy waiting to get to the pump must have thought I was taking too long because he honked his horn at me."

The next time I needed gas, I took my own Nielsen ratings by polling viewers.

"I actually do watch TV while I'm pumping gas," said Mike. "I like the weather, even though I'm outside and I already know what it's doing."

"Do you watch TV at home?" I asked.

"Not much," Mike said. "But I like comedies. 'The Big Bang Theory' is my favorite."

"If a sitcom was on TV at the gas station, would you watch it?" I inquired.

"It might take a while," Mike said, "but my car has a big tank, so maybe I could see the whole show."

Melanie said she watches the weather.

"I like the news, too," she added. "It's nice to know what's going on in the world. I just saw a report on gas prices."

This piqued my interest so much that I decided to talk with Violet Ivezaj, vice president of business operations for Gas Station TV, which is headquartered in Detroit. I thought of driving there from my home on Long Island, but I would have used too much gas, so I called her.

"You could have watched a lot of TV on the way out," said Violet, adding that Gas Station TV started in 2006 at five gas stations in Texas and is now in more than 3,000 stations across the country.

When I told Violet about my ratings poll, she said, "I'm glad people like us. We offer a lot of programming, like ESPN, AccuWeather, CNN, and Bloomberg. We're driven to make pumping gas a good experience."

"Driven?" I replied. "Nice one."

"Thank you," Violet said. "We want to have a positive impact."

"I don't think I'd use the word 'impact' when talking about cars," I noted.

"Oops," she said. "Let me put it this way: Millions of people are all pumped up over us."

"They must be tankful for Gas Station TV," I offered.

"Tankful?" Violet replied. "Nice one."

"Thank you," I said, adding that I have noticed that GSTV also has advertising for the products sold at gas stations, such as snacks and soda.

"We not only want to be entertaining and informative," Violet said, "but we want customers to buy merchandise from our clients."

"Have you ever been on Gas Station TV?" I asked.

"Not yet," said Violet. "My husband and children think I should be."

"Maybe you should get an agent," I suggested.

"You could be on," Violet said.

"That's a great idea," I responded. "If Gas Station TV starts a talk show, I could be the host. I can just imagine the promo: 'Watch Jerry and get gas.'"

CHAPTER 8

"How to Babysit a Grandma"

Over the river and through the woods to grandmother's house we go.

Chloe doesn't have to take such a circuitous route to visit Sue because our house is on a residential street and, besides, at fifteen months old, Chloe can't drive.

But she knows how to babysit Sue when she comes over because I got her a new book called, appropriately enough, "How to Babysit a Grandma."

The book, a New York Times bestseller, was written by Jean Reagan, who authored "How to Babysit a Grandpa," which has been enormously helpful to both me and Chloe.

Sue, who should be the subject of a book titled "How to Babysit a Husband" because without her I would be either dead or in prison, loves the grandma book.

"It's adorable," she told me after reading it.

"How to Babysit a Grandma," delightfully illustrated by Lee Wildish, opens with a little girl's parents dropping her off at her grandmother's house.

"When you babysit a grandma, if you're lucky ... it's a sleepover at her house," it begins. "What should you do when you get to her door? Put on a disguise and say, 'GUESS WHOOOOOO?'"

The girl is shown wearing a Groucho Marx disguise.

"That's what I am going to get for Chloe," I told Sue.

"Don't you dare," she retorted.

The best part of the book is "How to Keep a Grandma Busy."

Among the suggestions: "GO TO THE PARK. Bake snickerdoodles. Have a costume parade. GO TO THE PARK to feed the ducks. Do yoga. Look at family pictures. GO TO THE PARK to swing. ... GO TO THE PARK to slide. ... GO TO THE PARK to take photos."

"Chloe loves it when I take her to the park," Sue said.

"You mean when she takes you," I corrected.

"Right," said Sue. "She especially loves the slide and the swings."

The next part of the book is about the sleepover, which features lots of fun things for the girl and her grandma to do, such as making dinner ("Add sprinkles to anything") and finding places to sleep ("In a tent, on the floor, on the couch").

The final part takes place the next morning, when it's time to leave.

"How to Say Goodbye to a Grandma: Let her borrow some sprinkles, some books, some stickers, some ribbons. Say 'I love you!' without making a sound. Give her a BIG hug and ask, 'When can I babysit you again?'"

"I'm glad your wife liked the book," Reagan said when I called her to talk about it. "I wanted to make the grandma fun, as I'm sure Sue is. And I know Chloe thinks you're fun."

"She sure does," I replied. "People have often asked me if I spoil her. I say no, that's Sue's job. My job is to corrupt her. I told Sue I'm going to get Chloe the Groucho disguise. She didn't think it was a good idea. But when Chloe gets a little older, I am going to introduce her to the Marx Brothers and the Three Stooges."

Chloe already loves books, even though she can't read yet. So Sue and I read to her when she comes over or when we go to her house.

I haven't read my books to Chloe because they are below her intellectual level, but I did read both the grandpa and grandma books to her.

"What did she think?" asked Reagan, who is not a grandma yet.

"She loved them," I said. "She pointed to the slide and the swings in the grandma book. But for some reason, she seemed to understand that the grandpa needed a little more help."

"Next time she comes over," Reagan suggested, "she can help Sue babysit you."

"My Mother, the Plumber"

As a man who has regularly plumbed the depths for column material but doesn't know how to plumb a sink to get rid of even worse material, I recently faced a flood of problems that threatened to turn the laundry room into a scene from "Titanic."

So I called Rosina the Plumber.

Rosina, in case you need her services, is my mother.

Momz, as she is lovingly known in our family, isn't a plumber by trade. She had a long and rewarding career as a registered nurse, so she knows about human plumbing. Now that she's retired, she has been taking care of the plumbing in her house, the difference being that she doesn't have to take its blood pressure, dispense medication, or put up with complaints.

"One time," Momz recalled, "I dropped an earring down the sink."

My late father, the original and best Jerry Zezima, was the handiest guy I ever knew. He could have solved the problem, but he was at work, so my mother had to fish the earring out herself.

"I took off the elbow of the pipe under the sink," she said. "And there was the earring. It wasn't expensive, but I didn't want to lose it."

"If you had," I told her, "you could have said it was from the van Gogh collection."

"Another time," said Momz, "the bathtub got clogged up with soap and bath oil. I wasn't sure if I needed a snake or a plunger, but the guy at the hardware store said to pour this stuff down the drain. It didn't work. So I got a long brush with black bristles. I threaded it down the drain and — bingo! — the clog was gone."

I told her about the problem I was having with the sink in the laundry room.

"A hose from the washing machine empties water into the sink, but the sink is clogged and today it overflowed," I said. "I thought we were going to have an indoor swimming pool."

"Did you put on your bathing suit?" my mother asked.

"No," I replied. "But I did stick a piece of wire down the drain. It didn't work."

"Do you have a snake?" Momz wondered.

"Yes," I said. "Fortunately, it's not the poisonous kind or I'd need COBRA health insurance."

Momz politely ignored the remark and said, "Stick it down the drain."

"I tried," I said, "but it won't fit."

"Take the elbow off the pipe under the sink," she advised, "and run the snake through from there."

"You don't make house calls, do you?" I asked.

My mother, who lives in my hometown of Stamford, Connecticut, two hours from my house on Long Island, said, "Yes. And, unlike other plumbers, I wouldn't charge you. But you should take care of this right away. I know you can do it."

I was skeptical, so I drove to a nearby Home Depot store and went to the plumbing department, where I spoke with an associate named Charlie, who said, "Your mother is absolutely right."

"Could she work here?" I asked.

"We'd love to have her," Charlie responded.

I went back home and took the elbow off the pipe under the sink. Then I ran the snake through and pulled out about half a ton of wet lint and soapy residue.

When I had finished, Sue did a load of wash. The water went down the drain perfectly.

I called my mother to tell her the good news and to say that Home Depot could use her services.

"I'm going to stay retired," she said. "But maybe I could be a consultant. Who says you can't get a good plumber anymore?"

"My Mother, the Model"

My mom's the very model of the modern modeling mother. And she could soon share a runway with Heidi Klum and other model moms because she (my mother, not Heidi) began her modeling career recently at a fashion show in Stamford.

Heidi, who's forty-one, has gotten a lot more exposure, mainly because she's not shy about wearing lingerie in public. Besides, she began her career as a teenager.

My mom, who's a bit more modest, just turned ninety.

Because ninety is the new sixty, which happens to be my age, my mother was asked to take part in a fashion show at Chico's, a women's clothing chain with a store in the Stamford Town Center mall.

"I must have good genes," my mother said.

"Did you wear jeans?" I asked.

"No," she replied. "I had on a pair of boysenberry slacks."

"What about a top?" I inquired.

"I was wearing one," my mother assured me. "In fact, I wore a couple of tops."

"At the same time?" I wondered.

My mother sighed, because she knows I have a fashion plate in my head, and explained that first she wore a print blouse and then changed into another top with a coordinating jacket.

I was going to ask if she also wore the diamond-studded, $10-million bra that Heidi Klum famously sported on the cover of the Victoria's Secret catalog, but I thought better of it because Chico's doesn't sell stuff like that and this was, after all, my mother.

"But you could," I suggested, "be in the Chico's catalog."

"Yes, she could," said store manager Terry Mrijaj, whose name is pronounced "Terry."

"Do you know that my mother is ninety?" I asked when I called to talk about the new supermodel.

"She's amazing," Terry stated. "She's stylish, elegant, and beautiful. Whenever she comes in, customers remark on how great she looks in our clothes. She's a walking advertisement for the store."

Not bad considering my mom couldn't walk a year and a half ago, when she fell and broke her leg. But she has bounced back — she didn't bounce when she fell — and is driving again. And now, she's modeling.

"She's a natural," said Terry, adding that the fashion show, a breast cancer fundraiser, featured seven models, the youngest of whom is in her teens. My mom, not surprisingly, is the oldest.

Terry knows from experience because she was runner-up in the Miss Teen New York pageant when she was eighteen. "I'm forty-five now, so I'm half your mom's age," she said. "I hope I look that good when I'm ninety."

My mother said that when she was sixteen or seventeen, she was asked to model a sable coat at Levine & Smith, a fur shop in New York City.

"My father was so insulted — he didn't think modeling was very reputable — that he refused to let me do it and we never went back," my mother remembered. "So I went into nursing."

"Those white uniforms weren't too stylish," I noted.

"No, they weren't," my mother agreed. "I wear better clothes now."

They include the fringe skirt and black top she wore to a family birthday bash.

"How does it feel to be ninety?" I asked.

"Pretty good," she said. "I don't feel like it and I don't act like it."

"And," added Sue, who shares her birthday with my mother but is, of course, considerably younger, "you don't look like it."

Sue should know because she could be a model herself.

My mother's next gig will be another fashion show at Chico's.

"I know your mom will be a hit again," said Terry. "She's a star."

Let's see if Heidi Klum can say that when she's ninety.

CHAPTER 9

"Poppie Joins the Club"

In the grand scheme of things, there is nothing grander than being a grandparent.

I have been saying this to anyone who will listen, and anyone who won't, which encompasses everybody, since the birth of Chloe, who is about to turn two.

Now I can brag to even more people as a new member of the American Grandparents Association.

Membership in the AGA costs only $15 a year, all the better to save your money so you can buy toys and ice cream for your grandchild, who is not, let's face it, as wonderful as Chloe but must be pretty cute anyway.

According to the AGA website, grandparents.com, there are seventy million grandmothers and grandfathers in the United States. That includes Sue and yours truly, known to Chloe as, respectively, Nini and Poppie.

Imagine my surprise and delight when I found out that the chairman and CEO of the American Grandparents Association, famed rock music impresario Steve Leber, also is known as Poppie to his seven grandchildren.

"I love that name," Leber told me in a telephone conversation, adding that his late wife, Marion, was called Meme. "But it doesn't matter what your grandchildren call you. The best part of being a grandparent is when they look up to you."

"Chloe has to look up to me," I said. "She's not even three feet tall."

"There's a difference between being a parent and a grandparent," Leber said.

"Yes," I agreed. "And that difference can be described in one word: diapers. I have changed more of my granddaughter's diapers than I ever did for my two daughters, including Chloe's mommy."

"You have to change diapers," Leber said. "The funny thing is, it's not so bad when it's your grandchild. Unfortunately, I wasn't around too much when my three kids were young."

That's because Leber was frequently on the road, handling such artists as the Rolling Stones, Simon and Garfunkel, Diana Ross, the Jackson Five, the Beach Boys, and Aerosmith.

"But I've made up for it with my grandchildren," said Leber, adding that one of his proudest accomplishments was being the good luck charm for his grandson's soccer team.

"I was the mascot," Leber remembered. "And my second-oldest grandchild, Jack, was the star. The team was going for the New York state youth soccer championship. I missed a couple of games because I was in Florida and they lost. Everyone said to Jack, 'You have to get him back.' I came back and they won the state title. I became the trophy grandfather."

"Chloe is too young to play sports, although her daddy is a soccer fan," I said. "And I don't know if she considers me a trophy. But we have a special bond. She can be in her mother's arms, but when I walk into the room, she wants to come to me."

"That's because you're more fun," Leber said, adding: "You should never take your grandchildren for granted. Kids rebel against you, but not grandkids. They'll confide in you."

"And they won't be embarrassed to be seen with you?" I asked.

"Not like children are when they're growing up," Leber replied.

"I felt like a typhoid carrier," I recalled.

"Grandchildren will show you off," Leber promised. "They'll enjoy your company. It's great. You'll see."

I am already seeing it because Chloe enjoys my company and loves being seen with me. She doesn't even mind when I change her diapers.

"And now that you're an AGA member," Leber said, "you can get all kinds of discounts. That means you'll have more money to buy toys for your granddaughter."

"Thanks," I said. "But I'm already the biggest toy she has."

"Weather or Not"

I am frequently under the weather, but I seldom know whether I will weather the storm that forecasters have forecast, which is why I can't predict what kind of weather I will be under.

Still, as Bob Dylan famously sang, you don't need a weatherman to know which way the wind blows, which is fine with me because I am, according to people who aren't even weathermen, full of hot air.

So I recently spoke with the only guy in America who seems to know what the weather will be, not only tomorrow but as far ahead as two years from now.

He is Pete Geiger, editor of the Farmers' Almanac, the annual (since 1818) publication that correctly predicted the cold air that froze my shorts last winter.

"You should have worn long underwear," Geiger said from the Almanac's office in Lewiston, Maine, which is often chilly (the town, not the office, which is heated) even without the polar vortex that is expected to blanket the country again this winter.

"I guess I should have a blanket, too," I said.

"It would be a good idea," replied Geiger, who proudly added that the Almanac's weather forecasts are up to eighty-five percent accurate. "We don't have a groundhog," he noted. "And we don't use computers."

Instead, said Geiger, the forecasts are based on a secret mathematical and astronomical formula.

"What is it?" I asked.

"I can't tell you," he said. "It's a secret."

What Geiger could tell me was that the Farmers' Almanac relies, in part, on sunspots to help predict the weather. "And we almost always get it right," he said, "so that means we are sunspot on."

Geiger also predicted that he will live to a ripe old age because his father, Ray, was the editor of the Farmers' Almanac from 1935 to 1994, when he died at eighty-three.

"No editor in the history of the Almanac has died younger than that," said Geiger, sixty-three, who took over from his dad and has been the editor for twenty years. "It's my insurance policy."

"Instead of sunspots," I offered, "you can use liver spots."

"I spot a trend," said Geiger, adding that the Farmers' Almanac is "a guide to good living" and that the publication and its website, farmersalmanac.com, have "lots of great stuff."

Nonetheless, goes the old saying, everybody talks about the weather, but nobody does anything about it.

"We try," said Geiger.

"Try this," I said. "How come all these TV weather forecasters have satellites and computers and other sophisticated equipment and most of the time they still can't get it right?"

"I don't know," Geiger replied. "They ought to use woolly bear caterpillars and persimmon seeds."

"And why," I continued, "do they use all this silly jargon? They say things like 'partly' and 'variable.' It's just to cover their behinds, isn't it? And what's a 'forecast model'?"

"Vanna White," Geiger guessed.

"And how about 'heat index values'?" I wanted to know.

"I never heard of that one," Geiger admitted.

"Do you know what all meteorologists should have?" I said.

"What?" said Geiger.

"A window," I said. "Then they could just look outside and tell us what it's doing."

"Or maybe," Geiger suggested, "they could use the Farmers' Almanac."

"What's your favorite season?" I asked.

"Fall," Geiger responded.

"My favorite Season," I said, "is Frankie Valli."

Geiger said he also likes winter, but that he is getting "sick of it earlier" every year. "When we forecast a long one," he said, "people in town will high-five me. By March, they're booing me."

According to the Almanac's forecast, he won't get as many boos this winter, even though "shovelry and shivery" will be the bywords.

"It won't be as bad as last year," Geiger predicted, "but get out your shovel and be prepared to shiver. And that," he added, "is no snow job."

"Say It Ain't Snow"

Because I am a flake, and have been perpetrating snow jobs my whole life, I appreciate the wonders of winter.

The two things I wonder most about winter are: Why do some people throw away their snow shovels every year and have to buy new ones? And why do these same people go to the supermarket when a snowstorm is forecast to buy bread and milk when they never eat and drink those things when it doesn't snow?

I got some insight before a recent snowstorm from Chris, who works at a nearby home improvement store.

"Do you have a snow blower?" he asked.

"Yes," I replied, "but it doesn't work. It did work until we had a blizzard a few years ago, then it conked out. When I had it tuned up the following year, we didn't have any snow. Last year it worked fine. Now it's on the fritz again."

"Do you have gas?" Chris asked.

"You're getting a little personal, don't you think?" I said.

"I mean, did you put fresh gas in your snow blower?" Chris clarified. "Stale gas left over from last year can cause it to stall. You have to mix the new gas with oil."

"Do you have a snow blower?" I inquired.

"No," Chris admitted. "I have a two-year-old, and it was either buy a snow blower or pay for day care. So I bought a manual snow blower."

"What's that?" I asked.

"A shovel," Chris responded.

"How come, whenever it snows, people rush to a store like this to buy shovels?" I wondered. "Do they throw their snow shovels away at the end of winter and have to get new ones the following year?"

"I think they keep their shovels, but they put them in the shed and can't find them the next time it snows," Chris theorized. "The shovels move to the back of the shed and hide. Sometimes it happens in the garage. I think they have a union, and they have meetings where they decide how to outwit their owners and drive them crazy. The humans can't find the snow shovels, so they come here to buy new ones. It is," Chris added with a smile, "good for business."

At that moment, Sue came by.

"There you are," she said to me. "I couldn't find him," Sue said to Chris. "He's always getting lost."

"I can't help you there," said Chris. "But husbands are often told to get lost, so we're just following orders."

"We should buy a snow shovel," said Sue.

"We already have one," I noted.

"Do you know where it is?" Chris asked me.

"Yes," I said. "It's in the garage. I wedged it against the door so it couldn't hide."

Sue said we should get a second shovel. Then she said we should hurry up because she had to go to the supermarket to pick up some groceries before the snow started to fall.

"I hope you don't mean bread and milk," I said.

"No," Sue said. "We already have them."

"Why," I asked Chris, "do some people always rush out to buy bread and milk before it snows? If you go to their houses on a nice summer day, you'll never find them sitting at the kitchen table, eating bread and drinking milk."

"I don't know," said Chris. "I would think that before it snows, you'd want to buy beer. Or at least hot chocolate."

"Thanks for your help," I said to Chris before we headed for the checkout counter.

"You're welcome," he replied. "Make sure you put your new shovel in a place where it can't get away. And don't get lost yourself. After all, you're the one who'll have to get rid of the snow."

"The Hole Truth"

I am not a Rhodes Scholar because I have holes in my head, but I recently became a roads scholar because I learned how to patch holes in a road despite being suspended after only ten minutes on the job.

I earned my street smarts with the help of a terrific crew from the Brookhaven Highway Department, which kindly took me out on pothole patrol and allowed me to help smooth out a rough situation without once telling me that I was a pain in the asphalt.

That did not, however, prevent me from getting into hot water — actually, it was oil, which is used on the equipment — because I got off on the wrong foot by having the wrong footwear.

My day began at the town yard, where general foreman Dan Curtin assigned me to a crew that would perform pothole repair on a residential street in the hamlet of, appropriately enough, Rocky Point. Dan gave me a bright yellow vest, which was more stylish than my bland blue shirt and faded jeans, and a hard hat, which wasn't as hard as my head but which I had to wear anyway.

I was introduced to road crew worker Billy Lattman, who showed me the hot box attached to the truck we would be riding in.

"It holds four tons of asphalt that's heated to 290 degrees," Billy explained.

"I guess it's safer to think outside the box," I said.

"You're catching on already," said Billy, who drove with me to Asphalt Supply of Long Island to pick up three tons of the stuff.

"This past winter was one of the worst ever," said Billy, who has been working in the highway department for thirteen years and also is a volunteer fire chief. "So there are a lot of potholes to fill. And some of them are pretty big. I saw one with a hubcap in it. Another one had a bumper in it. It made me wonder what happened to the rest of the car."

"Do you have potholes on your street?" I asked.

"Yes," Billy replied. "We haven't gotten to them yet. My wife keeps asking when we're going to fill them in. I told her that we don't get any special treatment. But at least I've never lost a hubcap or a bumper in a pothole. I avoid them because I know where they are."

When we got to the work site, a narrow residential street named Friendship Drive, I met the rest of the personable and hardworking crew: Rob Nolan, John O'Sullivan, Gary Grob Jr., and Mario Desena.

I also met Tony Gallino, chief deputy of the Brookhaven Highway Department, who took one look at my ratty sneakers and suspended me.

"Not even ten minutes on the job and already you're suspended," Tony said, adding that I should have worn safety boots. "You're lucky the union won't let me fire you."

But Tony did compliment me on my work, which entailed shoveling hot asphalt into the ruts and potholes that pocked the street, smoothing it out with a long metal rake, and going over it with a roller.

"You're doing OK," said Tony. "Still, I wouldn't quit my day job."

I learned that the crew's day job is pretty tough. But they perform it with professionalism and good humor.

"You guys have real camaraderie," I said.

"That's because you're here," Billy responded. "We're on our best behavior."

It's a good thing I was, too, because at that very moment, Dan Losquadro, superintendent of highways, came by.

"I hear you've been doing a good job," Dan told me.

"I don't like to brag, but you see that spot?" I said, pointing to an area that I worked on. "I did that."

"Very nice," said Dan. "You are no longer suspended. I am reinstating you."

"Thanks," I said. "On the next job, maybe the crew can do something about the holes in my head."

CHAPTER 10

"Chloe and Poppie Go to the Aquarium"

Chloe, who just turned two, doesn't know yet that her Poppie is fishy. And it didn't seem to bother her that I'm all wet, too, when we took a trip to see some fine finny, flippered, feathered, furry, and flighty friends at the Long Island Aquarium and Exhibition Center in Riverhead.

Accompanying us on this exciting excursion were Lauren and Guillaume.

When we arrived on a weekday morning, a couple of seals were already up (they start work early) and looking for breakfast in their outdoor exhibit.

"They're gray seals," an aquarium staffer said.

"They should use Miss Clairol," I replied. "It would make them look younger."

"Do you know the difference between seals and sea lions?" she asked.

"The spelling?" I guessed.

"Well, yes," the staffer answered. "But seals don't have ear flaps."

"I suppose that means they don't wear earrings," I said.

"No," the staffer said.

"That's OK," I said. "They still have my seal of approval."

Chloe smiled.

Lauren rolled her eyes and said, "Come on, Dad. Let's go inside."

At the front desk, Lauren and Guillaume got in for free because they have an aquarium pass. Chloe also was admitted at no charge. My admission was $22.

"You could have gotten a senior citizen discount," Lauren said after I had paid with a card.

"I already gave you one," the young woman at the desk told me.

"Is it that obvious?" I asked.

"I do my job very well," she said as she handed me a receipt for $20.

Chloe took me by the hand and we capered off. The exhibit she liked best was the butterfly garden, where the colorful winged creatures flitted toward, past, and all around us. From overhead pipes came an occasional spray of water to keep the humidity level just right.

"I should have brought soap," I told another staffer. "Then I could take a shower."

Next door was the aviary, where playful parrots perched.

"This is for the birds!" I said to Chloe.

She giggled and took me by the hand again so we could catch up to Mommy and Daddy, who had made their way to the shark tank, watery home to all kinds of fish, including — what were the chances? — sharks.

"These are nurse sharks," I said. "There are no doctor sharks, but if you get bitten, you can sue and hire one of the sharks as your lawyer."

I also pointed out a clownfish.

"Who's a clownfish?" I asked Chloe.

"Poppie!" she answered correctly.

Then she led me through a couple of tunnels only big enough, supposedly, for kids. Outside, there was another tunnel, this one in the otter exhibit.

"There are two otters," I told Chloe. "The first one and the otter one."

Lauren and Guillaume groaned. Chloe giggled. Then she climbed into a child-size hot rod to pose for a picture.

Back inside, we saw stingrays, which were swimming in a pool.

"Do you know what all of them are named?" I asked.

"What?" said Guillaume.

"Ray."

"I'm going to throw you in there with them," Lauren said.

"I would be shocked," I retorted.

Chloe may not have understood the depth — we were, after all, in an aquarium — of Poppie's puns, but she was endlessly amused.

Then it was time for lunch. Chloe had her favorite: chicken nuggets and French fries.

"No fish?" I asked. "There are plenty to choose from."

When lunch was over, Chloe was tired, but she wasn't ready to go home. She wanted to have more fun.

"Go to Poppie," Guillaume told her.

"Poppie!" Chloe exclaimed as she jumped into my arms.

But it was, indeed, time to go, despite Chloe's protests.

"We'll come back," I promised her as we walked out. "And Poppie will bring some Miss Clairol for the seals."

"Gone Fishing"

If legendary composer George Gershwin had also been a fisherman, one of his greatest works might have been "Porgy and Bass."

I couldn't get the tune out of my otherwise empty head as I boarded the Osprey V, a charter boat out of Port Jefferson, for an afternoon of fishing for — you guessed it — porgy and bass.

What wasn't playing, in either my head or on board, was the theme from "Gilligan's Island," which would have been appropriate because the Osprey V is a sixty-five-foot Gillikin.

"Sometimes we play it as people are boarding," said Captain Amanda Peterson, "although we're not going out on a three-hour tour. It's four hours. And we won't strand you on an island."

"If the island had palm trees, I wouldn't mind," I said.

"Neither would I," said Captain Amanda. "But we're not going that far out."

We were, in fact, going only a few miles, to the Stratford (Connecticut) Shoal Light in the middle of Long Island Sound, prime grounds (or, rather, waters) for the aforementioned fish.

"If I catch a lot of them," I told Captain Amanda, "it would be a fluke."

"We're not going for fluke," she responded. "But you might catch a bluefish."

Captain Amanda, whose father, Captain Stew Cash, runs the business, is married to Captain James Peterson, who was officially piloting the boat on that day's excursion.

"I'm along for the ride," said Captain Amanda. "And to help you catch some fish."

I needed all the help I could get because it had been years since I last went fishing. I used to go with my father when I was a kid. Once, when I wasn't with him, he came back with a forty-one-pound striped bass.

"That's huge," said Captain James. "If you caught one that size today, you'd have a real fish story."

Captain James should know because he once caught an 873-pound tuna off the coast of Nantucket, Massachusetts.

"It was dressed," he said.

"In a bathing suit?" I inquired.

"No," Captain James replied. "I mean, the head and tail had been cut off. Originally, it weighed about a thousand pounds."

"That's huge," I said. "You have a real fish story."

I hoped to have one, too, and got off to a great start. Captain Amanda used clams to bait both hooks on my fishing pole. About ten seconds after I cast out, I felt a tug.

"You have a fish!" Captain Amanda exclaimed. As I reeled in, she added, "Two fish!"

On one hook was a porgy; on the other was a bass. The sea bass was puny, so Captain Amanda threw it back, but the porgy, which measured thirteen inches, three more than regulation size, was a keeper. So I kept it.

Good thing I did because I didn't catch another fish all day. Still, I had a fabulous time. I watched as the youngest fisherman on board, Kristian Tabala, four, with the help of his dad, Danny, reeled in a porgy that was bigger than mine.

"I'm gonna name him Bob," Kristian said.

"He's bobbing in the bucket, so it fits," I said. "What are you going to name the next fish you catch?"

Kristian thought for a moment and replied, "Rob."

The biggest catch of the day was a two-foot-long bluefish, hauled in by Vietnam veteran Chris Martinez, sixty-nine, the oldest of the twenty-six passengers. I was standing about five feet away.

"It could have been you," Chris said.

"On the hook?" I wondered.

"Then we would have had to cut off your head and tail," said Captain James.

As the Osprey V headed back, deck hand Travis MacRae did the same to my porgy. When he was finished, I had two nice fillets to share with Sue for dinner. They were delicious.

If only I had been standing five feet to my left, in Chris Martinez's spot, I'd be humming another Gershwin tune: "Rhapsody in Bluefish."

"The Call of the Wildman"

As a homebody whose idea of communing with nature is to open the windows, I could never see the forest for the trees, or even the mushrooms for the pizza, which is why I went on a nature walk with a guy who knows all about trees and mushrooms. He also makes his own pizza.

I naturally refer to "Wildman" Steve Brill, a naturalist who is a natural at taking people on nature walks, not just because he knows which mushrooms are good on pizza and which can kill you, but because for him, joking is second nature.

"I'm a funny guy," Wildman told me when we met at Belmont Lake State Park in West Babylon, New York. "And when I see mushrooms," he added, "I'm a fungi."

Like a fungus, Wildman's delightfully corny jokes grow on you, even though the twenty-five people who had signed up for the walk didn't see any corn.

"If you walk far enough," he told me, "you may develop corns."

Wildman, whose beard and mustache grow on him, and whose glasses and pith helmet make him look like a jungle professor, is billed as "America's Go-to Guy for Foraging." At sixty-five, he has seen the forage for the trees for thirty-two years, during which he has taken nature lovers and mushroom pizza aficionados on excursions throughout the Northeast.

He was even arrested by park rangers in 1986 for eating a dandelion while giving a tour in Central Park in New York City.

"I was charged with criminal mischief," Wildman remembered, adding that the case was eventually dropped. "I guess they were afraid I would eat the whole park."

There was no such concern on our walk.

"Will we see a lot of flora?" I asked Wildman as we got started.

"I don't think Flora is in this group," he replied, "but it would be nice to see a lot of her."

The first thing we saw was the common plantain, a lawn and garden weed that not only can be used on mosquito bites (you have to apply the juice to the affected area), but also can be eaten, as Wildman proved by producing some leaves he had cooked at home and passing them around so we could munch on them.

"I garnished them with parsley, sage, and rosemary," he said.

"Not thyme?" I asked, referring to the lyrics in the Simon and Garfunkel song "Scarborough Fair."

"That's Scarborough unfair," said Wildman, who also showed us a plant called Curly Dock. "Not to be confused," the Three Stooges fan noted, "with Moe Dock and Larry Dock."

Then we saw and tasted succulent, delicious wineberries. "They're dangerous because you can die of happiness," Wildman said as he popped some in his mouth. "They're berry good."

One thing that can kill humans is poison ivy, but only if you light it on fire and breathe in the smoke. "Do you know the only person who is immune to poison ivy smoke?" Wildman asked the group. When no one answered, he said, "Bill Clinton. He doesn't inhale."

Poison ivy flowers, Wildman added, are "beautiful but deadly, like my ex-girlfriend."

Then there are mushrooms, only about one percent of which are poisonous, such as amanitas. Wildman held one and said, "It's even worse for you than school lunch."

Most others, he added, are perfectly safe to eat, like the bolete we found.

"It's good with just about anything," Wildman said as he showed us a large specimen he had dug up from the ground.

"It's a 'shroom with a view," I offered.

"I'll have to remember that one," Wildman said.

His entire nature walk was memorable, the perfect combination of education and entertainment.

"I make foraging fun," Wildman said when the walk was over. Then he handed me a hunk of bolete to take home.

"It'll make a great mushroom pizza," he said. "Any way you slice it."

"Goodbye Kitty"

At the risk of starting a scandal involving promiscuous sex and teenage pregnancy, I have been living in a cathouse for almost two decades. And the madam of the establishment was the mother of nine children.

I refer to Kitty, one of a quartet of felines that have resided in my humble and frequently fur-flown household over the years. At the ripe old age of seventeen, the notorious party girl has gone to that big litter box in the sky.

Kitty became a member of the family in 1998, when Sue and I moved from Stamford to Long Island with Katie and Lauren; our original cat, Ramona; and our dog, Lizzie.

Not long afterward, I started getting strange phone calls at work.

"Meow," purred the voice on the other end.

"Who is this?" I said the first time it happened.

It was Lauren, who would have turned our home into Old MacDonald's Farm if she could have and was primarily responsible for Ramona, Lizzie, and the veritable menagerie of goldfish, frogs, hamsters, and gerbils we have fed, supported, and done everything for but put through college.

"What do you want?" I asked.

"A cat," Lauren replied.

"You already have a cat," I said.

"Ramona's an idiot," Lauren declared. "I want a real cat."

This went on for a couple of weeks until I finally relented.

"OK," I said. "Go get a real cat."

Lauren went to a nearby store — it wasn't a pet store — where the owner had placed in the front window a box that housed a litter of kittens. Lauren picked one and, at the cost of absolutely nothing, which was approximately what the cat was worth, brought her home. We tabbed her Kitty, even though she wasn't a tabby, until we could think of a better name for her. We couldn't, and Kitty started responding to it, so the name stuck.

Unfortunately, Kitty also started responding to cats of the opposite sex. Unlike Ramona, who was strictly a house cat — and probably too stupid to find her way home if we had let her out — Kitty was a nature lover.

One day, I got another call from Lauren, who had just turned sixteen.

"Guess what, Dad!" she said excitedly. "You're going to be a grandfather!"

I dropped the phone. When I recovered sufficiently to pick it up, I found out that Kitty was pregnant. In cat years, she was even younger than Lauren.

Kitty had a litter of four, two of which we found good homes for. The other two — a female Lauren named Bernice and a male she named Henry — got to stay in our home.

Do you think motherhood ended Kitty's wanton ways? Of course not. Shortly afterward, she was in a family way again. This time she had quintuplets, four of which were born one day under a bed. Kitty waited until the next day to have the fifth. I could have used a fifth myself.

We found good homes for all five kittens and took Kitty for a lady's procedure, even though she was anything but a lady. As a precaution, we also arranged snip jobs for Henry and Bernice, who were starting to have a sibling revelry.

Thereafter, Kitty's platonic affections were directed toward me, Sue, and anyone else she encountered, including Chloe, who loved to pet her. Kitty was sweet, smart, and small.

By contrast, Henry was practically the size of a mountain lion. He died at age twelve. Bernice, the sole surviving feline, eats like a mouse but is so fat she should have the word "Goodyear" emblazoned on her sides. She dwarfed Kitty, who ate constantly and wouldn't have flinched if you had set off a string of firecrackers right next to her while she chowed down.

Now that Kitty is gone, we have cut down considerably on the food bills. Still, we miss the old girl. She was — pregnant pause — the cat's meow.

CHAPTER 11

"Chloe and Poppie Go to the White House"

Since becoming a grandfather, I've really been on a roll. But nothing could top taking Chloe to Washington, D.C., for the White House Easter Egg Roll.

On Easter Sunday, I drove from Long Island to the nation's capital with Sue, Lauren, and, of course, Chloe. We stayed with Katie and Dave, who live and work in Washington.

Katie, a Washington Post reporter who had covered the White House (she's now on the campaign trail for the paper), got four tickets to the Easter Egg Roll, a national tradition dating back to the administration of Rutherford B. Hayes, whose wife, known as Lemonade Lucy, banned alcoholic beverages from the White House. In keeping with a family tradition, Katie and Dave had them at their house.

The next day — which was seventy-five degrees and sunny, with a refreshing breeze and no humidity, a rarity in D.C. — Chloe, Lauren, Sue, and I showed up at the waiting area, tickets in hand and ready to roll.

We had plenty of company. Over the course of the day, which began at 7:30 a.m., about 35,000 people converged on the White House grounds. We were in the last group — our time slot was 4:45-6:45 p.m. — but the line was still so long that we must have been in a different ZIP code.

At the checkpoint, Sue and Lauren had to empty their pocketbooks.

"I don't carry a pocketbook," I told one of the agents.

"That's OK, sir," he responded. "Empty your pockets."

He went through my wallet.

"Please don't harm the moths," I said.

He kept a straight face and handed it back to me.

Even Chloe's bag was searched.

"Those diapers aren't mine," I noted.

I'm surprised I wasn't arrested.

As we waited in line, Lauren asked an Egg Roll volunteer named Sheila if Peppa Pig, Chloe's favorite cartoon character, was still there.

"Yes," Sheila replied.

"How about President and Mrs. Obama?" I asked.

"They were here this morning," Sheila said.

"My granddaughter won't mind," I said. "She'll be more excited to see Peppa."

At that point, Chloe wasn't excited about anything. In fact, she was sleeping in her stroller.

A volunteer named Jean offered to write Lauren's phone number on Chloe's wrist band in case Chloe got lost.

"I'm always being told to get lost," I said. "Will you put my wife's phone number on my wrist band?"

"No," said Jean. "Nobody in your family is going to come and get you."

I felt sorry for Jean, who said she had been there since the gates opened that morning. "It's been a long day," she said wearily. "After this, I'm going home and having a cocktail."

"Where do you live?" I asked. "We'll join you."

"Come on over," Jean said.

After about forty-five minutes, we finally reached the South Lawn of the White House, which was swarming with excited kids, costumed characters, friendly volunteers, awestruck parents, and one confused grandfather.

The star of the show — Chloe, of course — woke up as we approached the Egg Roll area. I had the honor of accompanying her.

A volunteer named Carolyn handed Chloe a wooden spoon so she could roll an orange hard-boiled egg down a grassy lane about ten yards long. There were several other lanes, each with a spoon-wielding child and an adult.

The race was on. Or it would have been if I hadn't dropped the egg in front of Chloe and across the starting line before the whistle blew.

"I cheated, didn't I?" I said sheepishly.

"Yes, you did," Carolyn replied.

Then she blew the whistle. The crowd roared.

"Come on, Chloe!" I cried, showing her how to roll the egg with her wooden spoon.

She's only two, so she didn't quite get the hang of it at first, but she figured it out in pretty short order and — with help from Poppie — made her way toward the finish line. Sue and Lauren cheered her on.

Chloe didn't win, but she got the ultimate compliment from Carolyn: "We saved the best for last."

Only one thing could have been better — a photo op with Peppa Pig. Sure enough, the pink porker and her younger brother, George, were greeting their little fans in the shadow of the South Portico. Chloe hugged them both and posed for pictures.

At day's end, she was back in her stroller, holding a commemorative wooden egg signed by the Obamas' dogs, Bo and Sunny.

The little girl had the time of her life. So did I because, as Chloe would agree, that's the way Poppie rolls.

"Mr. Zezima Goes Back to Washington"

Before my recent visit to Washington, D.C., a town populated by clueless people, so one more wouldn't hurt, I had been in the nation's capital twice — once on purpose.

The other time, I took a wrong turn off the highway, found myself in Washington, and promptly got lost. Because the statute of limitations has expired, I can now admit that I violated federal law and asked another guy for directions. They did no good. It took three hours to find my way out of town.

I then realized that this is the reason the aforementioned clueless people are in Congress for so long: Even they can't find their way out.

In the best-laid-out city in America, the most important people are limo, cab, and bus drivers because they're the only ones who know where they are going.

To test this theory, I hailed a cab for an educational trip around town. Imagine both my chagrin and delight when I found out that my cabbie, a friendly twenty-seven-year-old guy named Yared, was on his first day on the job. I was his second customer.

"I don't know how to get around Washington," Yared admitted after I had buckled myself into the front passenger seat and he pulled away from my hotel.

"How did you get your taxi license?" I asked as he navigated the streets uncertainly.

"I used GPS," replied Yared, an Ethiopian immigrant who came to America eight years ago. "I live in Maryland because Washington is too expensive," he explained.

Before he became a cabbie, Yared parked cars.

"You must have wanted to take a step up and drive them," I said.

"Yes," Yared said when we were stopped at a red light and he consulted his GPS for the best way to get me back to the hotel. "I needed to make more money."

Approximately half a second after the light turned green, the guy behind us blasted his horn and Yared tentatively turned left onto a street whose name I don't know. Yared didn't seem to know it, either.

"You could be in Congress," I told him. "I'd vote for you."

"Thank you," Yared said with a smile.

We ended up making a big circle (or perhaps a trapezoid) back to the hotel. The fare came to $6.45. I gave Yared $10, told him to keep the change, and wished him luck in his new career. He thanked me again and drove slowly away.

Later, I spoke with Yared's first customer, Michelle Freed, a fellow scribbler who, like me, was in town for the annual conference of the National Society of Newspaper Columnists, an estimable organization that had to lower its otherwise high standards to let me join.

"He didn't know where he was going," Michelle said. "I didn't know where I was going and I had to give him directions. He was sweet, but it was just my luck that I got a cabbie who was on his first day on the job. I guess it was an honor to be his first customer."

That evening, on a bus ride to the Capitol, where the society had arranged to have dinner and bestow the Will Rogers Humanitarian Award (if you guessed that I didn't win, you would be right), I spoke with Robert Tabor, who said he has been driving a bus for thirty-seven years.

"Your backside must be sore," I suggested.

Robert chuckled and confirmed my theory that these guys are in Congress for so long because they can't find their way out of town.

"They don't seem to know where they are going even when they're not in Washington," observed Robert, sixty-four, who proudly said that D.C. has "the best transportation system in the country."

This isn't to say that he hasn't had his challenges as a driver.

"One time a guy got shot on my bus," Robert remembered, adding that the perpetrator was outside the vehicle. "The guy who got shot fell out. I closed the door and peeled rubber."

Robert, who said things have gotten much better in D.C. over the years, also noted that he has never been afraid to ask for directions.

"You know what this means, don't you?" I said.

"What?" said Robert.

"You can't run for Congress," I told him.

"That's OK," said Robert. "I can do more good driving a bus."

"A Connecticut Yankee in King Steven's Court"

As a Connecticut Yankee born and bred — or perhaps I should say born and white-bread, which is how most people think of Connecticut Yankees — I have always loved history, not just because I am old enough to be historical myself, but because I could never do algebra.

That's why I was so grateful when Joe Courtney, the Democratic congressman from Connecticut's Second District, defended our brave little state from the slander perpetrated against it in the 2012 film "Lincoln." The offenders were director Steven Spielberg, who is from Ohio, and screenwriter Tony Kushner, who is from New York, though they both might as well be from Neptune (and not New Jersey, either).

The movie showed how the president (William Henry Harrison — sorry, I mean Abraham Lincoln) pushed for the passage of the 13th Amendment, which abolished slavery.

In the key voting scene, two of the three members of the Connecticut delegation were wrongly depicted as voting against the amendment. In reality, there were four members and they all voted for it.

Incredulous after seeing the movie, Rep. Courtney wrote an open letter to Spielberg, pointing out the flub and asking for a correction on the DVDs, which the director had promised to send to middle and high schools across the country, presumably so the lie about Connecticut could be perpetuated for the current generation of students.

The letter prompted a snotty, half-baked response from Kushner, who threw Spielberg under the horse and buggy by saying the director approved the intentionally erroneous scene because it gave the audience "placeholders" (was he planning a dinner party?) and was a "rhythmic device" (which would have been more appropriate if he had been making a movie about George Gershwin).

Kushner also said he and Spielberg wanted to show how the closeness of the vote was the "historical reality." Truth be told, the historical reality was that they got it wrong on purpose. How stupid was that?

It had to be the biggest mistake of Spielberg's career, not only because it was easily avoidable and completely unnecessary, but because the resultant controversy was probably the main reason why he, Kushner, and the film itself didn't win Oscars in 2013.

Now that it's 2015, the 150th anniversary of the passage and ratification of the 13th Amendment, Rep. Courtney is again coming to Connecticut's defense.

This time he and his staff have produced a resource guide titled "Honoring Connecticut's Role in Abolishing Slavery, 150 Years Later." Intended to accompany any school showing of "Lincoln," which probably would put kids to sleep anyway, the guide shows how the state's four representatives — Augustus Brandegee, James English, Henry Deming, and John Henry Hubbard — braved hardships and personal attacks to vote for the 13th Amendment when it passed on January 31, 1865.

"Did they sail from Connecticut to Washington on their yachts or did they drive BMWs?" I asked Rep. Courtney in a phone conversation.

"I think they rode horses," he responded.

"Spielberg would be shocked," I said. "The photos of the four representatives in your guide show that they didn't wear polo shirts, so I assume they weren't wearing khakis and boat shoes, either."

"Probably just woolen suits," Rep. Courtney said.

"Another Connecticut myth exploded," I declared.

Unlike Spielberg, Kushner, and the late, great singer Sam Cooke, whose 1960 hit, "Wonderful World," opens with the lyrics, "Don't know much about history," Rep. Courtney, sixty-one, was a history major at Tufts University and graduated in the class of 1975.

"I wouldn't say I was magna cum laude," he acknowledged, "but I got pretty good grades."

"Do you think Spielberg and Kushner got good grades in history?" I asked.

"Based on what they did to Connecticut in 'Lincoln,' they might have flunked," said Rep. Courtney.

"I'm glad you set the record straight with your guide," I told him (it can be accessed at courtney.house.gov). "In fact, it would make a great movie."

"I can see it being a documentary," Rep. Courtney said.

"And I have just the guys to make it," I said. "Steven Spielberg and Tony Kushner."

"I don't know about Kushner," Rep. Courtney said.

"You're right," I replied. "He's a brilliant writer, but he never met a fact he didn't hate. How about if I wrote it and you produced it?"

"If you can find an agent and a backer," said Rep. Courtney, noting that politics in Hollywood are even worse than they are in Washington, "it could work."

"And if Spielberg promises to get it right this time, he can direct," I said. "Who knows, he might even win an Oscar."

CHAPTER 12

"What's in a Name? Ask Poppie"

I have been called many things in my life, not all of them repeatable in polite company, which I am seldom in anyway.

But the one I love to hear repeated is Poppie, which is what Chloe calls me.

Sue, who is called nothing but good things, especially by me, because without her I would be a four-letter word ("dead"), is known to Chloe as Nini.

I'm glad Sue and I have such wonderful grandparent names because we could have been called a lot worse.

I found this out when I saw that two fine family-oriented groups, BabyCenter (which provides advice on pregnancy and parenting) and the American Grandparents Association (which is what it sounds like), have each come out with a list of names that grandmothers and grandfathers are called these days, whether they like it or not.

At the top — or, if you prefer, the bottom — of the grandfather list is PeePaw. No offense to any guy whose grandchild calls him by that name, but I can't imagine Chloe saying to me, "PeePaw, I have to go pee-pee."

Then again, Poppie is perilously close to that post-Pampers potty predicament (and besides, it sort of rhymes), so maybe PeePaw isn't so bad after all.

Then there's Chief, which is considered a trendy name for grandfathers but sounds more like what Jimmy Olsen called Perry White in the 1950s "Superman" TV series. It conjures the following exchange:

Chloe: "Hey, Chief, pass me the coloring book."

Me: "Here you go, Honey. And don't call me Chief!"

A great grandfather name (though not a great-grandfather name) is the unlisted and presumably unique moniker bestowed on David Wright, not the New York Mets slugger but a professional window cleaner who cleaned the windows at our house: Granddude. For a goateed guy who used to be both a lawyer and a monk, it fits.

My buddy Tim Lovelette, who has four granddaughters, has two grandfather names, both on the AGA list: Big Daddy and Grumpy.

"Both are pretty accurate," Tim once told me.

His wife, Jane, also is known by two names on the AGA list: Go-Go (she's a marathon runner) and Grammy (I didn't know she could sing, but I eagerly await her first album).

If Jane becomes famous, she'll join other celebrities on the AGA list, including Donald Trump, who is known to his grandchildren — with great affection, I am sure — as Mr. Trump.

I can just imagine one of his grandkids sitting on his knee, running tiny fingers through his comb-over and asking, "Mr. Trump, will I be a hair to your fortune?"

On the grandmother side is Martha Stewart, who is called, simply, Martha.

I'm sure she would recommend using fine china to serve Count Chocula to your perfect little grandchild. And, in a pinch, she'd probably pass along this creative tip: "If you run out of Huggies, a doily will do."

There are no celebrities on the BabyCenter list, but there are some pretty creative grandparent names.

For grandmothers: Gramma-Bamma ("Gramma-Bamma, would you read me 'Green Eggs and Hamma'?"), Safta ("Do I Safta go to bed so early?"), and Yumma ("Yumma, Yumma, your cookies hit the spot in my tumma!").

For grandfathers: Bumpy ("Get in your carseat, it's gonna be a Bumpy ride"), Coach (at bedtime: "Put me in, Coach"), and Koko ("I'm cuckoo for Koko!").

If I can help it, Chloe will never see these lists. But she'd no doubt agree that some grandparent names are better than others.

Take it from Nini and Poppie.

"No Thanks for the Memory"

I am so technologically challenged that Chloe, who isn't even three years old, is more advanced than I am. I know this because she can use an iPad. I don't have an iPad, or an iPod, or even an iWatch, although I do have an iPhone and, according to my dentist, iTeeth.

Still, my constant battle with technology wouldn't be so bad if I could remember the approximately one hundred and forty-seven different passwords I need to perform all the tasks crucial to survival in the modern world, such as responding to those generous people in foreign lands who have notified me that I could inherit huge sums of money if I will send them my personal information, which unfortunately I can't access because I don't know the password.

For help and guidance, I spoke with Joe Guzzello, the manager of editorial systems in my office, where his technological expertise, positive attitude, and deadpan humor have saved many computer-crazed employees — including yours truly — from jumping out windows that don't even open.

"People are always asking me what their password is," Joe said sympathetically. "And I always tell them, 'How do I know? It's your password.' The problem is that there are so many passwords that you can't remember them all."

"How many passwords do you have?" I asked.

"Well over a hundred," Joe responded. "I have them in my phone."

"What if you lose your phone?" I wondered.

"I have a spreadsheet," Joe said.

"What if you can't find the spreadsheet?" I inquired.

"Then I'd be in the same boat as everybody else," said Joe.

"You'd probably need a password to start the boat," I suggested.

"The thing to remember," Joe said, "is KISS."

"I kiss my wife all the time," I replied, "and it still doesn't help me remember all my passwords."

Joe shook his head and said, "KISS stands for Keep It Simple, Stupid."

"I'll have to remember that," I noted, "because when it comes to remembering passwords, I'm really stupid."

Joe explained that choosing, for example, the name of a pet, or one of your children, or your favorite sports team, and adding a number representing, say, your birthday, will make the password easier to remember.

"But we're always told not to use the same password for everything, so you have to come up with different ones for your home computer or the one at work or doing your banking," I complained. "Then, when you have to change one of them, you can't use any of the previous dozen."

"That's where keeping it simple helps," Joe said. "Some people think their passwords have to be twenty-five characters long. That's wrong. Just tweak the ones you have."

Nonetheless, he acknowledged, keeping it simple can be pretty complicated.

"It was a lot different when I was growing up," said Joe, who's fifty-five. "Back then, all I had to remember was my locker combination."

No such luck for his daughters, who are eighteen and fifteen.

"In school, there aren't many textbooks anymore, so the kids have to do most of their work on iPads," Joe said.

"And they need passwords," I said.

"Right," said Joe.

"What are they supposed to tell the teacher if they lose their work: 'The dog ate my iPad'?" I asked.

"They can ask me," Joe said. "I have all their user names and passwords."

"User names are other things you have to remember," I noted. "So are PIN numbers. They're as bad as passwords."

"And when people can't remember them, I get called," said Joe, adding with a sigh: "It's not easy being me."

Joe, who's also a volunteer firefighter and a happily married man whose wife, he admitted, isn't too tech savvy, smiled and said, "Modern technology can be a beautiful thing, but it can also drive you crazy."

"I was already crazy," I said. "And I still can't remember all my passwords."

"Just keep it simple," Joe repeated.

"I have the perfect solution," I said. "I'll come up with a password with the name 'Joe' in it. And if I forget what it is, I'll know just who to call."

"What's the Bad Word?"

I know clichés like the back of my hand and I've always thought that people should avoid them like the plague.

That's why I am happy, at this point in time, to know that, going forward, two distinguished word gurus are thinking outside the box and, at the end of the day, fighting the good fight to keep the English language free from hackneyed phrases that I can't wrap my head around because, after all, it is what it is.

I refer to Tom Pink and John Shibley, who work at Lake Superior State University in Sault Ste. Marie, Michigan, and have come out with their annual Banished Words List.

Pink, director of the public relations department, and Shibley, PR writer and photographer, describe themselves as "co-conspirators" of the list, which this year includes such annoying words and phrases as "fiscal cliff," "kick the can down the road," "bucket list," "double down," "trending," and "YOLO," which stands for "you only live once."

Since Pink and Shibley are trending, I decided to double down and — spoiler alert (which also made the list) — call them because, of course, YOLO.

"I'd like to have some talking points with you guys," I said.

"You mean you want to discuss the Banished Words List?" asked Shibley, adding that "talking points" made the list in 2006.

"That's affirmative," I replied. "I have a few suggestions that, at the end of the day, should go on the list."

"Like the phrase 'at the end of the day'?" asked Pink, who said it was banished in 1999 but that "people keep using it."

"That's just one of them," I said.

"We always welcome new entries," said Shibley, noting that people can go to the Banished Words website, lssu.edu/banished, and make their own suggestions.

"I'd like to nominate 'going forward' and its equally evil twin, 'moving forward,' which have the language going backward," I said.

"They made it in 2001," Pink informed me.

"I can't wrap my head around it," I said.

"If you tried," Shibley said, "you'd get a headache."

"Then I wouldn't be able to think outside the box," I said.

"It's better than thinking inside the box," Shibley pointed out. "You might suffocate. I'd poke holes in the box. In fact, Tom and I poke holes in everything we read or hear. Our language needs some fresh air."

"We all have our linguistic annoyances," Pink said. "One of mine is 'preplanning.' It's like planning to plan. Or 'preregistration.' If you have to register before an event, when do you preregister — before the event is even planned?"

"Then you'd have to preplan," I said. "How about recipes that tell you to 'preheat' the oven before cooking dinner?"

"As opposed to turning it on afterward?" Pink asked.

"Exactly," I said. "Of course, if your dinner is on sale at the supermarket, you'd be getting a good price point."

"Good point," said Pink.

"It is what it is," I noted.

"That one got on in 2008," said Pink, who called the Banished Words List an "unpopularity contest," adding: "We try to have fun with it."

Said Shibley, "We're looking for good, witty nominations. Even if there's a word or phrase that has already made the list, you can nominate it again so it will get back on. We want input, which made the list, that is ongoing, which also made it."

"At this point in time," Pink said.

"That one was on the original list in 1976," said Shibley, who added that he and Pink appreciated my interest in joining the fight to rid the English language of the annoying words and phrases that have so negatively impacted (which made the list) our talking points.

"At the end of the day, I'm happy to help," I said. "Going forward."

"Talking the Talk"

When I was about twelve years old, my father and I had The Talk. It was such a traumatic experience that I remember only two things about it:

First, my father told me that what the birds and the bees did (though not with each other) was "more fun than playing football." I now realize that, unless you're a little kinky, you don't have to worry about concussions.

Second, my Aunt Anita (my father's sister, who was a real pistol) called in the middle of The Talk. My father excused himself and went into the kitchen. I strained to listen to what he was telling her, sweating in fear and embarrassment that Aunt Anita knew I was being filled in on the birds and the bees. It was the worst part of the whole thing.

"Today" and "Morning Joe" co-host Willie Geist never had to go through this excruciating father-son ritual because his father, "CBS News Sunday Morning" correspondent and legendary humorist Bill Geist, never bothered to subject young Willie (or himself) to The Talk.

It's all explained in Bill and Willie's hilarious and poignant book, "Good Talk, Dad: The Birds and the Bees ... and Other Conversations We Forgot to Have."

I wasn't embarrassed to have a brief conversation about the birds and the bees with Bill and Willie before their appearance at the 92nd Street Y in New York City, where veteran journalist Mike Barnicle moderated a vastly entertaining program in front of about three hundred Geist fans.

"You're one of the first people we've met who has actually had The Talk," Bill told me.

"There's anecdotal evidence that you should avoid it at all costs," added Willie.

"I never told Willie about the birds and the bees because I was afraid he'd correct me," Bill explained. "And I never understood why it's the birds and the bees. Why not two dogs in the backyard? Bees do it in midair and then the male dies."

Another conversation they never got around to having when Willie was a kid was the one about drinking.

"We did have it eventually," Bill said.

"A couple of weeks ago," added Willie, who's thirty-nine.

"You can't tell an eight-year-old about the dangers of vodka," said Bill, who's sixty-nine. "They don't understand."

Still, Bud Light gave a teenage Willie the courage to share a rooftop kiss with a girl in his high school class. That girl, Christina, is now his wife.

After Willie turned thirty, he went on a road trip to Atlantic City to see a Rolling Stones concert with his Uncle Herb, aptly named because he has worked in the herbal supplement business for years. Uncle Herb has a shrine to the Stones in the basement of his house in my hometown of Stamford. It would not be giving too much away to say that the trip was memorable because some of it can't be remembered.

"I couldn't keep up with Herb anymore," Bill said, "so Willie had to take up the slack."

Not all the stories in "Good Talk, Dad" are about fun and games. A couple of years ago, Bill finally opened up to his family about his service in Vietnam, where he was a combat photographer. "Until then, I didn't even open up to myself," Bill said. "Denial has always worked for me."

A few years ago, Bill finally discussed with Willie and daughter Libby what his wife, Jody, had long known: Bill has Parkinson's disease. "I didn't want the kids to worry about me," he explained.

That didn't stop Bill from getting a laugh out of his condition. Speaking at a gala for the Michael J. Fox Foundation, he began by saying, "I thought at times about ending it all." The audience at New York's Waldorf Astoria sat in stunned silence. "But," Bill continued, "I was afraid that if I tried to shoot myself, I'd miss."

The program at the 92nd Street Y was sensational, not surprising considering that the book and its authors are, too.

Afterward, I confessed to Bill that I never had a father-son talk with my kids about the birds and the bees, either.

"It was easy to get out of," I said. "I have daughters."

CHAPTER 13

"The Royal Treatment"

Since the birth of the little princess, people around the world have been abuzz with excitement.

I refer, of course, to Chloe.

People seem excited about Princess Charlotte, too.

That goes for the royal family, but it also goes for my family because Guillaume refers to Charlotte's big brother, Prince George, as "my future son-in-law."

And now Chloe and George could get a chance to meet. According to published reports, the royal family is renting a mansion for the summer in the Hamptons, the tony towns that are a birthstone's throw from my family's home, the Zezimanse.

"I think Chloe and George would be perfect for each other," said Patrick McLaughlin, a licensed broker for Douglas Elliman Real Estate in East Hampton, my second-favorite Hampton after Lionel. "They're a little young yet," McLaughlin added, "but I have no doubt that one day it will be a marriage made in heaven."

I have no doubt, either. As I explained to McLaughlin, Guillaume and Lauren were married in the South of France in 2011, one day after George's parents, William and Kate, were married in England. That made the royal couple the opening act for the real Wedding of the Century.

After I wrote to William and Kate to congratulate them, I got a lovely letter in return, thanking me for my good wishes and wishing Lauren and Guillaume the best.

When George was born in 2013, four months after Chloe, I sent a congratulatory letter to Prince Charles, from one grandfather to another.

He must have been all ears, because he sent me a postcard of himself and his lovely wife, Camilla, as a token of his appreciation.

Naturally, the Zezimas were ecstatic when Charlotte was born, though we know that Chloe is the true princess.

"That's safe to say," McLaughlin noted. "I can see why George would be eager to meet her."

In addition to selling and renting real estate to the rich and famous, whose identities are his little secret, McLaughlin writes a whimsical blog for Hamptons Chatter, a website that contains chatter about — you guessed it — Grand Forks, North Dakota.

No, I mean the Hamptons.

"I have fun with it," said McLaughlin, who posted a piece about the rumored royal visit.

It began: "The royal formerly known as Prince William, now known as Kate Middleton's husband, is apparently planning to bring his Windsor brood to spend their summer in the Hamptons! I know! I know! I'm as excited as the next Anglophile!"

I'm excited, too! And not just because of McLaughlin's propensity for using exclamation points!

"Hi, William," he continued. "Hopefully, you didn't buy that real estate yet and you'll be calling me as your agent in the near future."

McLaughlin offered some suggestions about must-see spots in the Hamptons.

"One of them is Cyril's, a great dive bar," McLaughlin told me.

"I've been known to frequent dive bars," I said. "Maybe William and I could have a pint of ale."

"Then," McLaughlin suggested, "you could take him to Home Goods. That's another place he absolutely has to see."

"I'm sure Kate would love to shop there," I said.

"And she'd get great bargains," said McLaughlin, adding that the royal family simply has to visit Martha Stewart, who has a home in the Hamptons. "She loves drop-by guests," he noted.

"Do you think Martha would love it if I dropped by?" I asked.

"I'm sure she would," McLaughlin said. "She might even bake you a cake."

But the real highlight would be a royal visit to my house.

"It's not technically in the Hamptons," I said. "But it has a nice backyard with a slide and a kiddie pool."

"Chloe and George aren't old enough for cocktails by the pool," McLaughlin said, "but you could serve them juice in sippy cups."

"It's a little too early to start planning a wedding," I said. "But I know it'll be love at first sight."

"On the Fence"

I have never believed the old saying that good fences make good neighbors because, really, who wants to live next door to a guy who deals in stolen merchandise?

Fortunately for me and Sue, the neighbors on both sides of us are friendly, law-abiding citizens.

Still, we needed a new fence because the two front sections of the old one were rotting, sagging, and generally in deplorable condition, which our neighbors are too nice to say about me.

So we called Suffolk Fence Company of Port Jefferson Station. As its name implies, the company specializes in fencing (not with swords, thank God) and offers an array of styles, all of which come with doors that don't, like the one on our old fence, have to be held up by ropes.

At nine a.m. on a sunny Saturday, Herberth and David arrived to install our new fence.

"I've been here before," said Herberth, who remembered coming over several years ago to replace a side-yard fence that was crushed when one of our trees fell on the house next door.

"The tree crashed through the roof of the garage," I said. "Fortunately, we have good neighbors. Their insurance company covered the damage and they got a lot of free firewood."

"My father-in-law says that when a hurricane is coming, you should go up on the roof and rip it up, then call the insurance company and say, 'I need money.' Of course, he's only kidding," said Herberth, who kidded me about my Three Stooges T-shirt. "I used to watch them in Spanish when I was growing up in El Salvador," he recalled.

"I can just imagine Curly saying, 'Buenos dias. Nyuk, nyuk, nyuk!'" I said.

Herberth pointed to the image of Moe on my shirt and said, "He's the smart one, but he's really pretty dumb."

"Can you imagine if the Stooges installed fences?" I said.

"It would be crazy!" Herberth exclaimed.

Just then, David walked by, playfully flipping a hammer.

"If it hit him in the head, it would be funny," Herberth said.

"If it hit me in the head," I added, "he'd need a new hammer."

"Just like the Stooges," said Herberth, who asked if we have a dog.

"We used to," I replied, "but she went to that big backyard in the sky."

"I wanted to make sure that if you had one, she wouldn't get away when we took the old fence down," said Herberth, adding that his dog used to dig under the fence at home. "She'd go over to my neighbor's house for a visit. My boss gave me a fence, which was very nice of him, but I had to put another one outside the den door so the dog would have her own area."

Herberth has had his share of both dog and people trouble on the job.

"One time I was taking a customer's fence down and his neighbor got angry. He said he was going to send out his pit bull so it could eat me," Herberth remembered. "I said, 'Go ahead. I have a hammer.' I love animals and would never hurt one, but I wanted to see what this guy would do. It turned out that he didn't have a pit bull, just this little dog that was pretty cute. One other time, a little dog bit me on the knee, but it was cold and I was wearing thermal pants, so it didn't break the skin."

"Do good fences make good neighbors?" I asked.

"I don't know," said Herberth, who has been on the job for thirteen years. "I have good neighbors. So do you. But some people don't like their neighbors. One time I had to put a four-foot-tall section of lattice on top of the fence we had installed so this guy's neighbors couldn't look over and see him."

Herberth and David took down the two old sections of fencing, which were made of wood, and installed new ones, which are PVC. They worked hard and did a fantastic job.

"That looks much better," I said.

"It's a good fence," Herberth noted. "I guess that makes you a good neighbor."

"When the Bough Breaks"

When I bought my house, which the bank owns but kindly allows me to pay for, I was thrilled to have a big yard with lots of beautiful trees. Apparently, the trees don't feel the same, which is why, after a recent storm, the oak was on me.

Not literally, of course, because if a tree fell on my head, it would be crushed to kindling, while my head would be slightly dented but otherwise unharmed.

This particular tree either was hit by lightning — I was shocked, SHOCKED, that such a thing could happen — or had its uppermost branches sheared off by what some meteorologists speculated was a tornado, not likely because I don't live in Kansas, even though, according to the bank, there's no place like home.

Fortunately, mine wasn't hit by the tree, which nonetheless knocked out my power. It knocked out my house's power, too, when a huge branch fell and came to rest on a power line in the backyard, threatening to plunge the entire neighborhood into darkness, especially at night.

Then again, the setting sun does the same thing all the time. Good thing I don't have solar power.

Anyway, it took two weeks for the power company to come over and cut down the offending branch and another huge one that had almost entirely snapped off the trunk. That branch was resting against a neighbor's tree on the property line and would have taken down the power line if it had fallen, too.

During those two weeks, the power was restored but went off twice more, both times when the sun, which also rises, was shining brightly and there was nary a breeze, save for my hot air.

When the crew from the power company finally arrived and felled the two big branches, Sue was told they couldn't be cut up and hauled away, but one guy said he could do it privately for a price that could have bankrupted Donald Trump.

So I got an estimate from Vinny, who works for O'Connell's Landscaping, the company that cuts what little grass we have. The lawn looks like a stretch of Death Valley because the trees in the front and back yards are so shady.

"I'm kind of shady myself," I told Vinny.

"Maybe I should cut you down," he replied with a smile.

Vinny, forty-one, a Navy veteran who served in the Persian Gulf, said I was lucky the tree didn't fall on my house.

"If it had," I noted, "at least I'd have hardwood floors."

"I've seen plenty of trees that fell on people's roofs and into their pools," said Vinny, adding that he slept through the storm. "It didn't affect me, and I live only a few miles away. I guess the worst of it was in your neighborhood."

Vinny surveyed my branch-littered backyard and gave me a reasonable price to cut up the wood and take it away.

"I'm a geezer with a handsaw," I said. "I could never do it myself."

"You don't have to," said Vinny, who, a few days later, sent over three of his best men: Efren, William, and Mario.

"You have a lot of rot," said Efren, the supervisor of the crew.

"I know," I responded. "But what about the tree?"

"It has rot, too," said Efren, who showed me and Sue the decaying wood in one of the branches.

"I used to like oaks," I said. "Now I hate them. Never mind the acorns. It's the brown gunk they drop in the spring that's the worst. And they're supposed to be the strongest trees, but every time a breeze blows through, the yard is littered with twigs. Now this."

"And it could happen again," Efren said as William and Mario finished the job.

"You know what they say," I told him. "Everything happens in trees."

"The Lord of the Rungs"

I have never climbed the corporate ladder because I have acrophobia, which is an irrational fear of being any higher off the ground than the top of my head.

But business must be booming for millions of guys who aren't afraid of climbing to the tops of houses like mine, a two-story Colonial that could give a mountain goat nosebleeds, because I have noticed that most of the trucks and vans on the road these days have ladders on them.

The economy may be down, but ladder sales seem to be up. My buddy Tim Lovelette has a theory about the rise of the ladder industry.

"Everyone has at least one ladder, which lasts for eternity, and everyone dies," Tim explained. "At the point of death, these ladders need to find their way to new owners. That's one of the big reasons for yard sales. Yet, hardware stores worldwide continue to sell new ladders. There has to be a point in time where ladders will outnumber people."

Tim suggested that the world is "ladder happy" and said we must be approaching the point where we can't even give ladders away.

"Considering that we have more ladders than are needed, there must be some sort of secret ladder subsidy buried in legislation somewhere that supports the manufacture of new ladders," Tim said. "Perhaps it's coupled with our foreign aid programs. Are we dumping ladders on Third World countries simply to support new ladder manufacture here? If that's the case, we're really headed for trouble. In a global ladder race, the Chinese will beat us every time. We'll have developing nations full of starving people and ladders."

Tim acknowledged that he has a philosophical bent because he majored in philosophy at Saint Michael's College in Colchester, Vermont, where he and I were in the notorious class of 1975. He also said that, like me, he has a great fear of heights.

"I think that's the reason I didn't attain the lofty distinction of graduating magna cum ladder," Tim said. "I was a step down at cum ladder."

The last time Tim was on a ladder, he said, was in 1974.

"Jane and I were just married and living for the summer in a rental house on Cape Cod," said Tim, a Massachusetts native who married his high school sweetheart in junior year of college. "A friend of mine gave me a television antenna. Yep, it was the Dark Ages: No cable. In any event, I got to this little ranch-style house, set up the ladder, and installed the antenna on the roof. Now comes the good part: I couldn't get off the roof. I was on that roof for well over two hours before I could muster the courage to get back on the ladder. I could have jumped off the roof and not injured myself, it was that low. It was at that point that I gave up my lifelong ambition to be Batman."

Tim added that he doesn't know where he got the ladder.

"Outside of a stepladder, I don't own one," he said. "But don't mention that to anyone. I'm afraid people will find out and start dumping their excess ladders on me."

That would be the second-worst thing that could happen to Tim, or to me, or to anyone with a fear of heights.

The worst thing, according to Tim, would be a home improvement Armageddon.

"I had been satisfied with thinking about how the world will end," Tim said. "It was the old question: Will it end by fire or ice? I guess the answer was right in front of my face and I was blind to it. I'll be a son of a gun if God didn't orchestrate the whole thing back when the universe was created. The world will end in ladders."

"They've Got My Number"

Not many people know this, because I just made it up, but when Alexander Graham Bell made the first telephone call, to his assistant, Thomas Watson, and said, "Watson, come here, I want you," he heard a voice on the other end say, "This isn't Watson. You have the wrong number."

Thus began a long, irritating chapter in telephonic history involving millions of clueless people who wrongly call other people who often respond in such an unmannerly fashion that the caller has no choice but to unwittingly call back in a futile attempt to reach a third party who, by this time, could well be dead.

I recently received wrong-number calls from three people who were not only apologetic but so pleasant that our conversations could have been (if the callers hadn't sensed that they were talking to an idiot) the beginning of beautiful friendships.

The first call was from a woman named Carol. After I said, "Hello," she said, "How are you, Mitch?"

"I'm fine, thanks," I replied. "There's just one problem."

"What's that?" Carol said tentatively.

"This isn't Mitch."

"Oh, I'm so sorry!" Carol exclaimed, adding that she was actually calling her friend Fran, who is married to Mitch. "I don't have Fran's cellphone number, so I called Mitch," Carol said.

"I'm Jerry," I said.

"Nice to meet you," said Carol, a retired nurse who lives in New York. "Mitch and Fran live in Florida," she told me.

"What's their number?" I asked.

"I wish I knew," said Carol, who noted that she sometimes gets calls from people who have the wrong number. "I try to be nice about it," she said.

"Me, too," I said, relating the story of how we used to get calls for a pizzeria. "This went on for months. Finally, I started taking orders. I don't know if they're still in business."

Carol laughed. "Nice talking to you," she said.

"You, too," I replied. "Give my best to Mitch."

A couple of days later, I got a call from a guy named Frank, who was trying to reach his son, also named Frank, who, like Mitch and Fran, lives in Florida.

"Maybe it's a Florida thing," I told Frank, who apologized when he realized he had misdialed.

"It happens," I said, introducing myself.

"I should know my son's phone number," Frank said. "I guess I got the area code mixed up."

"I'm frequently mixed up," I said, "even when I'm not making phone calls."

"I know how you feel," said Frank. "Thanks for the chat."

"You're welcome," I responded. "Good luck reaching your son."

A few minutes later, the phone rang again.

"Frank?" said the familiar voice on the other end.

"Frank?" I replied.

"Jerry?"

"Yes."

"I did it again!" Frank cried. "I don't know what to do, but I'm going to get to the bottom of this."

He must have because he didn't call back.

The next day I got a call from a woman named Anita, who asked if I wanted to be an altar boy at a nearby church.

"I'm a kid at heart, but I'm probably a little too old to be an altar boy," I said.

"My goodness, I must have the wrong number," said Anita, adding that she's a secretary at the church and was calling families in the parish to recruit altar boys.

"I wouldn't want the church to get hit by lightning," I said.

"I don't think that would happen," Anita said.

"I wasn't exactly an altar boy when I was young enough to be an altar boy," I confessed.

"You sound like a good person," said Anita. "And we're always looking for new parishioners. We'd love to have you."

"If I decide to become an altar boy," I said, "I'll call you."

"OK," said Anita. "Just make sure you don't dial the wrong number."

"Home Alone"

If Hollywood wants to make another "Home Alone" movie, this time with the Macaulay Culkin character all grown up but no more mature than he was as an eight-year-old in the 1990 original, I would be happy to take the role.

That's because I was recently left home alone for the weekend.

Sue, without whom I would have starved to death long ago, went out of town, leaving me to my own devices. Fortunately, the devices included a corkscrew, if I wanted some wine, and a bottle opener, if I wanted some beer. I had both, though not at the same time because even I know that if you go too crazy on the libations while you are home alone, and happen to lock yourself outside or start a kitchen fire and can't find the phone to call 911, or realize, as the house burns to the ground, that you forgot to buy marshmallows, there is no one there to help you.

In fact, there is no one there to do anything with you. Dismiss the notion that you will have a wild party. When the cat's away, the mice will not play. I am a man, not a mouse, and the only creature that kept me any company was our cat, Bernice, who is — I say this with great affection — a total moron.

To make sure I wasn't bored, Sue left me a list of things to do, including the crucially important chore of watering the garden.

"Did you remember to do that?" she asked when she called, presumably to see if I was still alive.

"Yes," I told her proudly. "I was so excited, I wet my plants."

I could hear Sue's eyes roll in their sockets on the other end of the phone.

Still, I wanted a little time to myself, which wasn't difficult since I was alone anyway, so I drove into town to buy a cigar.

When I got to the cigar store, I asked the owner, Julio, if his wife had ever left him home alone.

"Yes," he said.

"What did you do?" I wondered.

"I took out the garbage and watched a lot of sports on TV," said Julio, who will celebrate his twentieth wedding anniversary in October.

"That's a biggie," I noted. "Don't forget it."

"I did forget our anniversary once and my wife wasn't happy," Julio said. "Now I write it down on the calendar. If I forget it again, she might leave me home for good."

Outside, I met Frank and Denise, who have been married for twenty-eight years.

"Has your wife ever left you home alone?" I asked Frank.

"Once," he said.

"What did you do?" I asked.

"I went to Puerto Rico," Frank answered.

"What a swell idea!" I exclaimed. "But I don't have time. My wife will be home tomorrow."

"Make sure you clean up after yourself," Denise advised. "You don't want your wife coming home to a mess."

"I've been making messes for the thirty-seven years we have been married," I said. "But I'll try to make sure the house is nice and neat."

When I got home, I went outside, climbed into a hammock with a beer and a cigar, and enjoyed some quality time with myself.

Afterward, I heard the familiar strains of the neighborhood ice cream truck. I went around front and bought a toasted almond bar from Chris, who has been on the same route since the 1970s.

"Does your wife ever leave you home alone?" I asked.

"Yes," replied Chris, who has been married for forty-eight years.

"What do you do?" I inquired.

"Eat, work, and sleep," he said. "Some guys fool around."

"Not me," I said.

"Me, either," said Chris, who admitted that he doesn't do household chores while his wife is away.

"I do," I said. "In fact, I have to go inside and do them before my wife gets back. But I'll tell you this: The next time she leaves me home alone, I'm going to Puerto Rico."

CHAPTER 14

"The Ice Cream Man Cometh"

In the whole wide world — which, as NASA has proven, is a whole lot wider than Pluto, a Disney character who can't hold a candle to "Sesame Street" star Elmo — nothing is sweeter than Chloe.

The only thing that comes close is ice cream. So it was especially sweet when Chloe, who's a big Elmo fan, met Christos Skartsiaris, our neighborhood ice cream man.

Chris, who has driven his truck on the same route for almost forty years, pulled up in front of my house on a warm weekend afternoon, the annoyingly repetitive strains of "Zip-a-Dee-Doo-Dah" mercifully silenced when he turned off the ignition.

"Doesn't listening to that song over and over drive you crazy?" I asked. To which Chris responded, "What song?"

As I peered into the open side window of the truck, I saw not only the extensive selection of frozen treats but a small gallery of photos.

"My grandchildren," said Chris, who has four, with one on the way.

"They're beautiful," I said. "I'm a grandfather, too. My granddaughter should be here any minute. She's not driving yet because she's only two."

"That will happen soon enough," said Chris.

"As I have told people who aren't grandparents: If you think your kids grow up fast, wait until you have grandchildren," I said.

"Tell me about it," replied Chris, whose grandchildren — Nico, eight; Logan, eight; Sophia, five; and Dylan, four — are growing up fast because, in part, they are nourished with ice cream.

"They'll ask me, 'Papou, can I get something from your truck?' Of course, I always say yes," said Chris, whose wife, Joan, is called Yaya.

"Chloe calls me Poppie," I said, adding that Sue is Nini.

"Kids these days are really smart," Chris said. "I had a hundred-dollar bill recently and Nico said, 'Papou, can I have this dollar?' I said, 'Sure, if you give me $99 in change.' He smiled because he knew it wasn't a dollar."

"Nico could be my accountant," I declared.

"I wasn't that smart when I was eight," said Chris.

"I'm not that smart now," I conceded.

Just then, Chloe pulled up with Lauren, Guillaume, and Maggie the dog.

"Poppie!" Chloe squealed when she saw me.

Lauren brought her over to the truck and introduced her to Chris.

"Hello, beautiful girl," Chris said as he scooped (he is, after all, an ice cream man) Chloe into his arms.

"Say hi," Lauren urged Chloe.

"Hi," Chloe said tentatively.

Chris put her down and showed her his rolling office. Chloe was fascinated.

"She's like a kid in an ice cream truck," I said.

Chris asked what she wanted.

"I-keem!" Chloe exclaimed.

Lauren suggested a Jolly Rancher push-up pop, a rainbow-colored treat with cherry, watermelon, and green apple flavors.

"What do you say?" Lauren asked Chloe when Chris handed her the pop.

"Thank you," Chloe said.

"You're welcome, sweetheart," said Chris, who propped her on the window ledge.

Chloe sat there and ate her ice cream, smearing it on her mouth like lipstick and licking it off.

"Here's another one," Chris said, handing it to Lauren. "For later."

He also gave ice cream to the rest of us.

"It's on me," Chris said.

At that point, it also was on Chloe, who couldn't quite keep up with the melting treat.

"Looks like Mommy has to do laundry," Chris observed.

Then he started up his truck, "Zip-a-Dee-Doo-Dah" ringing once more through the neighborhood.

"Say bye," Lauren said to Chloe.

"Bye," Chloe said.

"And thank you."

"Thank you."

After dinner, Chloe went to the front door, looking for the truck.

"I-keem," she said.

Chloe had made a friend. And he's sweet, too.

"Now That's Italian!"

As a nice Italian boy, as well as a former runner-up in the Newman's Own & Good Housekeeping Recipe Contest for a dish I called Zezima's Zesty Ziti Zinger, I have many remembrances of things pasta.

Aside from being a flash in the pan, however, I can barely boil spaghetti. So I took a class in which I learned how to make ravioli.

The class, at the Brookhaven Free Library, was given by Richard Kanowsky, whose last name isn't Italian and whose immediate family is as culinarily challenged as I am.

"My mom is horrible in the kitchen," Chef Richard said. "My dad, too."

But his maternal grandmother was "a really good cook," he said. "I learned from her."

Although Chef Richard's ethnic background includes Russian, German, Dutch, French, and Czech, his grandmother was half-Sicilian. "It qualifies me to make ravioli," he said.

"My ethnic background includes Martian," I told him. "Otherwise, I'm Italian. My mom is a great cook. My wife and my mother-in-law are of Italian descent. They're great cooks, too. Unfortunately," I added, "it doesn't qualify me to make ravioli."

"We'll fix that," promised Chef Richard, who was impressed that I beat out all but one person in a field of thousands in the national recipe contest. "What was your secret?" he asked.

"Red wine and vodka," I responded. "Paul Newman loved my dish. I told him I fed some to my dog to see if it was all right. He asked if my dog was still alive. When I said yes, he wolfed the stuff down like he hadn't eaten in a week. That he and my dog have since passed on is merely a coincidence."

After going over his professional background — he has cooked at the Ritz-Carlton in Boston and at Carnegie Hall in New York City and co-owns Kanobley Catering on Long Island — Chef Richard told the dozen class members that we would be rolling in dough.

"That," he explained, "is why I asked you to bring rolling pins."

Although Chef Richard had already made the dough we would be using in the class, he demonstrated how it's done so we could do it at home. The ingredients were flour, eggs, olive oil, heavy cream, and kosher salt. The process involved making a well, or a large hole in the middle, and using a fork to stir the egg mixture into the flour and collapsing the well walls.

"You knead the dough," Chef Richard noted.

"No kidding," I said to Toni Anne, who was sitting next to me. "I ought to play Powerball."

After Chef Richard gave us eggs, cheese, flour, and bags of dough, he handed out powdered rubber gloves and showed us how to roll pieces of dough, cut them into smaller pieces, squeeze a small mound of cheese onto each piece, use a pastry brush to apply the beaten eggs to the edges, and fold over the dough, using our fingertips to push air out of the ravioli.

"If there's an air pocket," he said, "the ravioli could explode in boiling water."

Chef Richard went around the class to inspect our work. When he got to me, he said, "Your ravioli could be served in a restaurant."

"Tell the Ritz-Carlton I'm available," I said.

Then I took my dozen ravioli home to cook for myself and Sue.

I plopped them into a pot of boiling water. They didn't explode. I drained them, put them in a bowl, covered them in tomato sauce, and served a ravioli to Sue.

"Delicious," she said. "It didn't break apart. You did a good job."

Coming from a great Italian cook, it was the ultimate compliment. Paul Newman would have loved it.

"Breakfast at Zezima's"

Beer: It's not just for breakfast anymore. But the greatest beverage in the history of mankind, which guys often use to hook up with womankind, is the perfect accompaniment to the first meal of the day.

I found this out after making a recipe for Scotch Egg, which I got from "The American Craft Beer Cookbook," the fabulous culinary and libational bible by a guy with the best job on the planet, beer writer John Holl.

For strictly journalistic purposes, I decided to talk with Holl about his laudable purpose in life, which is to spread the gospel of beer. So I met him after work at Alewife, an estimable establishment in Long Island City that serves vast varieties of the aforementioned brew.

"Millions of guys would give their right arms to have your job," I told Holl, adding that they'd then have to drink beer with their left hands.

"It's not as glamorous as you might think," he replied. "I don't go out carousing. In fact, sometimes I'm in bed at ten or ten-thirty at night. In Seattle, on my book tour, I was sitting in a hotel room with the curtains closed, eating olives out of a box. Still," Holl added with a smile, "it's not a bad gig."

The dedicated journalist showed that he has a nose for brews by sniffing a Riprap Baltic Porter and commenting on its nutty aroma. I proved to be a little nutty myself by emulating Holl and ending up with a schnoz full of foam.

Next we tried a Medula, an English Imperial IPA, which like the first beer is made by the Barrier Brewing Company of Oceanside, New York.

"It smells like Juicy Fruit gum," said Holl.

"Except you can't chew it," I noted.

What we could chew was dinner, which we ate at the bar. Holl ordered a salad (fewer calories, less filling) and I had a burger (just the opposite). Holl suggested another Barrier beer, Rembrandt Porter. Like the painter, it was a Dutch treat.

"It goes well with meat," said Holl, who had a lighter brew with his salad.

"I once made my own beer," I told him. "Jerry's Nasty Ale."

"How was it?" Holl asked.

"It didn't kill me," I replied proudly. "It had a smoky flavor. I don't know why. I didn't put cigar ashes in it. But it was pretty good."

As responsible beer drinkers should always do, we paced ourselves and didn't overindulge. At the end of the evening, I told Holl I had decided to make Scotch Egg, mainly because the recipe came from Half Full Brewery in my hometown of Stamford.

"Besides," I added, "I've never had beer for breakfast before."

"An Irish stout goes well with eggs," said Holl, thirty-three, a warm, funny guy who has tried all the recipes in the colorful, 343-page book and is anything but a beer snob. "Let me know how it turns out."

A couple of days later, I bought a four-pack of Murphy's, an Irish stout that is imported by United States Beverage, also in Stamford. The next morning, I opened "The American Craft Beer Cookbook" to page ten, laid it on the kitchen counter, and commenced to make Scotch Egg.

"Please don't burn the house down," said Sue.

Easier said than done because somewhere around step three, as I was heating oil in a deep fryer and had turned my attention to removing pork sausage from its casing and simultaneously boiling eggs, the smoke alarm went off.

The phone rang. It was a nice woman from the home security company, calling to ask if I had burned the house down.

"No," I explained. "I'm just making breakfast. Want to come over for eggs and beer?"

"I'd love to," she said, "but I have to work."

Sue opened the windows to get the smoke out and I finished making breakfast. I put the spiced, sausage-wrapped eggs on a plate and dug in. They were delicious.

I washed them down with an Irish stout. After a cooking experience like that, I really needed it.

CHAPTER 15

"Poppie's Personal Trainer"

At the advanced age of sixty-one (my age is advancing while the rest of me is regressing), I am happy to say that I don't need to join a health club.

That's because I have a personal trainer: Chloe.

Chloe, whose age has advanced to two and a half in the blink of an eye (my other eye doesn't work as well as it used to), keeps me in shape like no professional ever could.

That was exhaustingly evident during a trip to Safari Adventure, a children's activity and entertainment center in Riverhead.

For me, a child at heart, which got a strenuous workout and pumped enough blood to actually reach my brain, the place was a gym where I had a one-day membership.

Ordinarily, Chloe keeps me going with activities such as playing hide-and-seek; running around the dining room table; pushing her in her toy car (she honks the horn) or on her tricycle (she rings the bell); having foot races in the backyard; making her fly like Supergirl; doing bench presses with her; carrying her; catching her as she goes down the slide; helping her go up and down stairs; taking her to the park and pushing her on the swings; playing catch; playing soccer; frolicking with her in the kiddie pool; jumping in puddles; or simply walking hand-in-hand to and fro wherever we may be.

If these were Olympic sports, I would have set the world record for gold medals and you would have seen me (and Chloe) on boxes of Wheaties.

As it is, I have already gone through a pair of sneakers since Chloe started walking, even though I don't see her every day, much to my chagrin because (a) I love her and (b) I could use the exercise.

I got plenty of it at Safari Adventure.

The first thing I had to do was take off my sneakers, which for once avoided wear and tear, even if my feet and the rest of me didn't.

Then Chloe led me to a huge inflatable slide. I thought she wanted me to watch her go down, but she had a better idea: She wanted me to go with her.

Getting to the top entailed going through a rubber obstacle course. I couldn't stand because I am too tall, so I had to crawl, which must have been a pathetic sight since I kept toppling over like I had been out on an all-night bender.

Chloe patiently waited for me as I caught up with her at the stairs, which she scampered up in a flash. It took me approximately the length of time it would have taken Chloe to read "War and Peace."

Then — whoosh! — down the slide she went. I followed, slowly and clumsily, suffering rubber burns on my elbows and knees in the process.

"Again!" Chloe said when I reached the bottom.

This exercise was repeated about half a dozen times until Chloe took me by the hand and led me to the bouncy house, where my conditioning reached a whole new level. Actually, two levels: up and down.

It is safe to say, though not safe to do if you are a cardiac patient, that Chloe got the jump on me. This was the routine: bounce, bounce, bounce, plop! Every time she did it, I did, too, which made Chloe giggle with delight.

If I had a dollar for every time we bounced and plopped, I could have paid off my mortgage.

Then Chloe led me back to the slide, then to the bouncy house again, then to another, even taller slide. At least this one didn't have an obstacle course.

After an hour and a half, Chloe was ready to go home. I was ready to go to the hospital. But it was invigorating, and fun, and I'd go back to Safari Adventure in a rapidly pounding, chest-exploding heartbeat.

Thanks to my little personal trainer, I'm in the best shape of any grandpa I know.

"The Tale of the Tape"

At the risk of being challenged to a fight by Sylvester Stallone, who could beat me with one hand tied behind his back (though I might have a chance if he were blindfolded, too), I am going to call my ongoing kidney stone saga "Rocky."

The boxing analogy is apt because the latest installment, "Rocky IV," had the following tale of the tape: If there is one thing worse than having a kidney stone, it's having your arm hair ripped out by the roots when an otherwise gentle nurse pulls the tape off your IV.

As a person who has had four kidney stones, I can say with experience, not to mention drugs, that you never really get used to them.

But it's the tape that sticks in my memory.

"Men hate it," said a very nice nurse named Janet, who took good care of me in the emergency room at John T. Mather Memorial (that word makes me nervous) Hospital in Port Jefferson.

Sue, who has always taken good care of me, drove me there when I had a kidney stone attack at four o'clock on a Saturday morning.

Janet dutifully hooked me up to an IV and started a drip that mercifully eliminated my pain, as well as a good deal of my cognitive functions.

When it was time to be unhooked, I looked up at Janet and said, "This is the worst part."

"I know," she replied sympathetically. "Some guys actually scream when I pull the tape off. And don't get me started on needles. I've seen big, burly men who are covered in tattoos, but when I get ready to put a needle in their arm, they moan and cry. One guy fainted. I always say, 'How did you get all these tattoos? From someone who used a needle.' Let me tell you something: Men are babies. If they had to give birth, the human race would die out."

"The first time I had a kidney stone," I recalled, "a nurse told me it was the male equivalent of childbirth. I said that at least I wouldn't have to put the stone through college."

Janet nodded knowingly. Then she took hold of the tape and said, "Ready?"

I winced and replied, "Let 'er rip!" I instantly regretted the comment, but by then it was too late. I shrieked and said, "The drugs aren't working anymore."

I also had tape on my other arm, from which Janet had drawn blood.

"Good thing I'm not an octopus," I noted.

Janet nodded again and repeated the tape removal.

"Sorry," she said. "But it's all over now."

Unfortunately, the kidney stone wasn't, so I made an appointment with my urologist, Dr. Albert Kim, who has an office in — how appropriate is this? — Stony Brook.

"This, too, shall pass," Dr. Kim predicted.

Sure enough, it did. I was extremely grateful because my three previous kidney stones either had to be blasted with shock waves or removed via a surgical procedure that's the medical equivalent of Roto-Rooter.

On a follow-up visit, the good doctor gave me a list of foods and beverages that I should or shouldn't eat and drink. Among the bad things are peanut butter, which I love, and beer, which I love even more. Also on the bad list are — you can't make this up — kidney beans.

Dr. Kim informed me that I have another stone in my right kidney, but that it's small and should pass, too.

When I told him the tale of the tape, he said, "Shave your arms. You don't want to get into another hairy situation."

"The Inside Story"

If there is one kind of doctor I could never be, it's a gastroenterologist. Aside from the fact that I'm a gasbag, the reason is simple: When it comes to invasive medical procedures that involve the exploration of cavities not treated by a dentist, I don't know which end is up.

Fortunately, my gastroenterologist, Dr. Emily Glazer, doesn't have that problem. That's why she could make both head and tail of my problem by performing an endoscopy and a colonoscopy on me at the same time.

It had to be one of the most remarkable feats in medical annals (not to be confused with a similar word that would be an appalling but appropriate typo, especially if my blood was type O).

During treatment for my most recent kidney stone, a CAT scan showed that I had an abnormality in my upper gastrointestinal tract.

"It'll be one-stop shopping," Dr. Glazer said of the double procedure as I sat in her office for a consultation.

"I don't like to shop," I replied.

"Trust me," she said. "You're getting a good deal."

The next evening, I had to prepare for the colonoscopy. I hadn't had one for at least a dozen years and was, according to Dr. Glazer, "long past due." The preparation involved the ingestion of a vile liquid that had the same effect on my innards as dynamite would have on the Hoover Dam.

Feeling flushed, I arrived at seven o'clock the following morning at Mather Hospital. Sue drove me there because I would be too loopy to drive myself home, not that such a state of discombobulation would be anything out of the ordinary.

The first thing I had to do was get undressed and put on a johnny coat, the flimsy gown that opens in the back, meaning I couldn't even turn the other cheek. Thankfully, I didn't have to because I got to put on a second johnny coat and wear it the other way around so I was fully covered. I hoped the insurance company would agree.

"Poor Johnny," I said to a nice nurse named Margaret. "I'm wearing both of his coats. He'll catch cold."

"Don't worry," she responded. "We'll take good care of him."

Margaret and everyone else at Mather took good care of me. When a catheter was hooked up to the back of my left hand, I asked, "Can I still wave to people?"

"Yes," Margaret said. "But they might move you to the psych unit."

Instead, I was moved to the operating room, where Dr. Robert Bernstein, the anesthesiologist, said I'd be getting a GI procedure.

"Are you sure?" I asked. "I'm not in the Army."

I could tell he couldn't wait to knock me out. But he said that first he would spray my throat with a local anesthetic.

"I don't care where it comes from," I said.

"It's to prevent a gag reflex," Dr. Bernstein explained.

"I'm always pulling gags," I told him.

"I can see that," he said.

Dr. Glazer came in and said the whole thing would take less than half an hour.

"We'll do the endoscopy first," she said, noting that the procedure would be done through my mouth. "After that, we'll spin you around and do the colonoscopy."

"You mean it will be like a spin class?" I asked.

"Yes," said Dr. Glazer. "Except you won't be awake."

A moment later, it was all quiet on the western front. In what seemed like another moment, I was awake again and lying in the recovery unit. I was, predictably, even loopier than usual. But considering the abnormality turned out to be the only thing about me that's normal, I did very well, thanks to the wonderful doctors and nurses who had a great deal of patience with the silliest of patients.

As I said to one of them before Sue drove me home, "It all came out in the end."

"Food for Thought"

According to an old saying, you are what you eat. Since I am full of baloney, I eat what I am.

Unfortunately, I don't know what to eat these days because I am on three different diets.

This has nothing to do with fat, which is all in my head. It stems from the fact that: (a) I have a history of kidney stones, (b) I have a history of high cholesterol, and (c) I aced history in high school.

Naturally, all three diets contradict each other.

The first one, which was given to me by my urologist, is called the Low Oxalate Meal Plan. I had never heard of oxalates, but they sound like a species of cattle ("The male oxalate, which can weigh fifteen-hundred pounds, is one of the dumbest animals on earth") whose meat makes an excellent steak that I could wash down with beer.

Imagine my horror when I, a guy who loves beer so much that my blood would probably come out with a head on it, saw that I'm not supposed to drink it (beer, not blood, in which case I would be a vampire whose only meals are midnight snacks).

The first item in the "beverages and juices" part of the Low Oxalate Meal Plan, under the heading "avoid completely," is: "Beer: draft, stout (Guinness), lager, pilsner."

But when I looked over at the list of good beverages, I saw: "Beer, bottled."

At that point I needed a beer, bottled, because I was on a diet that contradicted even itself. At least I could use it to wash down an oxalate steak because beef is among the meats that are OK to eat.

I could also have beef with red wine, which I am not surprised is on the good beverage list because I have long considered it over-the-counter heart medicine.

Speaking of which, my second diet is called the Heart Healthy Meal Plan and is designed to lower my cholesterol.

I got the diet from a nurse who took my blood pressure and measured my cholesterol during a wellness fair at work.

Before I was put on medication, my cholesterol levels looked like an NBA score. Now, the nurse said, my good cholesterol is good (and very polite, I might add) and my bad cholesterol isn't good but isn't as bad as it used to be.

To make it better, I am supposed to follow the Heart Healthy Meal Plan, which contradicts the Low Oxalate Meal Plan because on the former I can eat peanut butter but not beef and on the latter I can eat beef but not peanut butter.

On my third meal plan, the High Fiber Diet, which I got from a nurse in a hospital where I had an endoscopy and a colonoscopy at the same time, I can have beans, which I am not supposed to have on the Low Oxalate Meal Plan, and I can have beef, which I can't have on the Heart Healthy Meal Plan.

I must admit that I am not a fan of vegetables, even though I am one, which makes it easy to ignore all three diets because I can have certain vegetables on one or more of them but not other veggies on one or more of either the same or opposing diets. So, to avoid confusion, as well as kidney stones, high cholesterol, and a heart attack, I won't eat them at all.

My favorite meal plan is the High Fiber Diet because it allows me to have any beverage I want. That goes for beer. Whether bottled or draft, stout (Guinness), lager, and pilsner, I don't know, but I am going to drink it anyway.

If you're on a diet these days, it's the only thing that makes any sense.

"Just What the Doctor Ordered"

By the time you read this, I could be dead. If so, I am going to get a second opinion.

Fortunately, that shouldn't be necessary because I got a first opinion from my doctor, who not only said I probably won't die in the next five years but predicted I will live to be a hundred and fifty-one.

I began to wonder about my longevity when I read that researchers in the United Kingdom had created a survey that can calculate a person's chances of dying in the next five years.

I took the fourteen-question survey, which inquired about my age (sixty-one), my gender (male), if I am married (yes), how many cars I drive (one at a time), practically everything except my underwear size (thirty-four, in case you can't afford to buy me another car), and the results were encouraging: My chances of dying in the next five years are only 2.7 percent and my relative age is fifty-three, which means I seem eight years younger, physically, than I really am. Mentally, I belong in kindergarten.

Soon after I took the survey, I went for a physical to Dr. Antoun Mitromaras, who has a practice in Port Jefferson Station.

"You are in excellent condition," Dr. Mitromaras said after examining me, perusing my blood test (good thing it wasn't an algebra test or I'd be on life support), and looking at my EKG. "Are you active?"

"If I were any less active," I responded, "I'd be in hibernation. Why?"

"Because," Dr. Mitromaras informed me, "you have the heart of an athlete."

"I hope it's not Babe Ruth," I said. "He's dead."

"You are very much alive," the good doctor declared.

"Speaking of which," I noted, "will I die in the next five years?"

"I don't want to say anything because you might get hit by an airplane," Dr. Mitromaras said. "But otherwise, you should be around for a long time. I predict you will live another ninety years."

"I'm sixty-one now," I said.

"That means," Dr. Mitromaras said, "you will live to be a hundred and fifty-one."

"Will you still be my doctor?" I asked.

"Of course," said Dr. Mitromaras, who is seventy-three. "Do you think I am going to die? Never!"

This was very reassuring because Dr. Mitromaras has impeccable credentials.

"In addition to being a physician," he said, "I am a head and neck surgeon."

"I'm a pain in the neck," I told him.

"I can fix that," he said.

"And my head is empty," I noted.

"Then I guess there is nothing to operate on," Dr. Mitromaras said.

"My heart is in good shape, but what I really need is a brain," I said, echoing the Scarecrow in "The Wizard of Oz."

"Maybe you can get a transplant," the doctor suggested.

"Here's what I really want to know," I said. "Have you ever seen those medicine commercials on TV in which the announcer says how good the product is, then spends the rest of the time warning how it can kill you?"

"Yes," Dr. Mitromaras said. "They're very entertaining."

"And the announcer always says, 'Ask your doctor.' Has anyone ever asked you about these medicines?" I wondered.

"Yes," Dr. Mitromaras said.

"What do you say?" I inquired.

"I say that if they can kill you, don't take them," he replied.

"Sound advice," I said. "The only thing I take is cholesterol medicine."

"It's working because your cholesterol levels are good," Dr. Mitromaras said.

"As they say in those commercials, after I take it, I shouldn't operate heavy machinery," I said. "You know, like a steamroller."

"I wouldn't drive one, especially in traffic, because you'd get high blood pressure," Dr. Mitromaras said. "Then you'd need more medicine."

"Thank you, doctor," I said as I shook his hand. "You are a credit to your profession."

"See you next year," Dr. Mitromaras said.

"And for the next ninety years?" I asked.

"Yes," he promised. "I'll be here."

CHAPTER 16

"Depth of a Salesman"

Despite the lamentable fact that I couldn't sell skis in Vermont during the winter, or surfboards in Hawaii during the summer, or even beer to castaways on a desert island, mainly because I would have consumed it myself, I recently got a job as a salesman.

I am not getting paid (and I'm worth every penny), but I do get hugs and kisses, which are priceless.

My boss is Chloe, who just started preschool and came home on her first day with — you guessed it — a fundraiser.

Fundraisers are an excellent way not only to raise funds for schools, but to deplete funds from the families whose children or grandchildren go to the schools that need to raise funds.

This is known, in many American households, as an economic downturn.

But if it helps kids, especially Chloe, I am all for it. Besides, I'd only blow the money on frivolous luxuries like food and shelter.

I remember when Katie and Lauren came home from school with fundraisers that Sue and I had to bring around the neighborhood and then take to work so friends and co-workers could buy stuff after we had bought stuff, thus ensuring that the girls wouldn't be known as the only kids in school with cheap parents.

Then, of course, Sue and I had to buy stuff from the kids of all those friends and co-workers, proving that we weren't cheap. During the school year, however, we were practically broke.

Now, after enjoying fundraiser retirement for the past two decades, I am back in the sales game.

Acting on behalf of Chloe, the CEO (child executive officer) of this enterprise, Lauren handed me the thirty-two-page sales brochure, titled "Prestige Gift Collection 2015," which offered "unique gifts, kitchen helpers, delicious treats and premium gift wraps."

The first person to whom I had to give a sales pitch was, naturally, myself.

"There's a lot to choose from," said Sue, who had already purchased several gifts, including Item No. 11, the Ho Ho Snowman Roll Wrap.

"I guess I don't have to buy wrapping paper," I said, though I was intrigued by Item No. 25, the Mystery Roll Wrap. Even more intriguing was Item No. 21, the Mystery Gift.

"What's the mystery?" I wondered. "You order them but they never arrive?"

"Pick something else," suggested Sue, who not only is a better shopper than I am but also, obviously, a better salesperson.

I perused the possibilities, including Item No. 29, the Sunrise Egg Mold ("If my eggs have mold, I'm not eating them," I told Sue); Item No. 42, the Snap-Lock Containers ("We already have enough Tupperware to store leftovers for Luxembourg"); Item No. 47, the Professional Knife Sharpener Wand ("I'd bleed to death"); and Item No. 66, Cashew Torties ("Isn't she an adult film star?").

I ended up getting a subscription to Sports Illustrated, so I could enjoy reading about people who are bigger, stronger, younger, and richer than I am.

Then I took the brochure to work.

One colleague said apologetically, "I don't even buy from my own kids."

Another one said, "I have to go to a meeting," and never came back.

Fortunately, several others fell for my irresistible sales pitch, which began, "I hate to ask this," and generously purchased items I knew they didn't need or want but bought anyway, probably because — and this is the key to salesmanship — they felt sorry for me.

I am proud and slightly flummoxed to report that I sold $87 in merchandise, which not only helped Chloe be tops in her class, but ought to make me Preschool Salesman of the Year.

"Do the Right Bling"

As a guy whose only piece of jewelry is a wedding ring and who thinks karats are what rabbits eat, I have never believed that it don't mean a thing if you ain't got that bling.

Now, however, I have a band of gold that even Sue would like.

Unfortunately, neither she nor anyone else can see it.

That's because it's in my mouth.

This exquisite piece is a fixed mandibular retainer, which was affixed to the back of my bottom teeth by Dr. Stephanie Shinmachi, an orthodontic resident at the Dental Care Center at Stony Brook University on Long Island.

I got it at the end of my five-year treatment at Stony Brook, where I had gone because two of my teeth — one on the top, the other on the bottom — had been pushed out of alignment. To straighten things out, I got braces.

This is not uncommon among baby boomers who, like me, did not have braces when they were young. How well I remember my unfortunate classmates who answered to the name "metal-mouth" and were warned, by sympathetic friends such as myself, to watch out for flying magnets.

I didn't have to worry about such calamities because I got invisible braces, which go by the brand name Invisalign and are made of clear plastic, unlike traditional braces that look like tracks on Metro-North or the Long Island Rail Road.

During my time at Stony Brook, I was in the capable and always gloved hands of three orthodontic residents: Dr. Ben Murray, Dr. Michael Sheinis, and, of course, Dr. Shinmachi. All of them deserve to win the Nobel Prize, not just for being able to shut me up for extended periods, but also for being brave enough to work in a vast and forbidding place that resembles the Grand Canyon with molars.

Dr. Murray, who was originally assigned to my case, graduated after two years of working on me. He was replaced by Dr. Sheinis, who also graduated after a couple of years of treating me.

Dr. Shinmachi took over for the final year of my treatment and finished what turned out to be a beautiful job.

"I'm like the last runner in a relay race," she told me during my final appointment. "Dr. Sheinis handed me the baton and I took it over the finish line."

"It's a good thing you didn't put the baton in my mouth," I said. "There's plenty of room for one."

Dr. Shinmachi was far too kind to agree, so she smiled (showing off perfect teeth) and said, "I'm going to give you a retainer."

"I'm not a lawyer," I said, "but I've been admitted to many bars. And I could use the extra money."

Dr. Shinmachi was talking about the clear, braces-like trays that would hold my teeth in place now that I was done with my Invisalign treatment.

"You can wear them at night while you're sleeping," she said.

"During the day I like to sleep at my desk," I replied. "Can I wear them at work?"

"Sure," said Dr. Shinmachi, adding that my other retainer, the mandibular one, will prevent my bottom teeth from relapsing.

"I call it gold bling," she said.

"Should I go to a jewelry store to have it appraised?" I asked.

"You could," she said. "Just don't try to hock it."

"Do you think my wife would like it?" I wondered.

"Yes," Dr. Shinmachi answered. "But it's not the kind of thing you'd want to get her for her birthday."

"I'll buy her a piece of jewelry that people can see," I said with my nice new smile. "And I'll put my money where my mouth is."

"Stubble, Stubble, Toil and Trouble"

When I was in high school and was just starting to shave, which led to so much blood loss that I should have been honored by the Red Cross, I read "The Razor's Edge," the W. Somerset Maugham classic that was not, much to my amazement, because I was a stupid kid, about shaving.

Young men reading the book today would be similarly surprised, which is why many of them, unwilling to risk bleeding to death, barely shave at all.

Lately I have noticed that stubble is in style. Everywhere you look, there are guys with five o'clock shadow.

I don't know what happens when the time changes and it's either six o'clock or four o'clock (spring ahead, fall behind, cut yourself, wounds to bind), but I do know that women love this look on young guys but hate it on geezers like me.

One of them is Sue, to whom I cuddled up on a rare day when I didn't shave.

"Stop it!" she shrieked when I nuzzled her with a face (mine, naturally) that looked and felt like sandpaper.

"Don't you like the rugged look?" I asked.

"No!" she cried. "Go away!"

So I did. The next day, after I shaved, I went to a store called The Art of Shaving for wisdom in what has become the lost art of shaving.

Because I didn't know where the store was in the mall, I violated the unwritten law that men should never ask other men for directions and asked Scott Molloy, who was manning the guest services desk, for directions.

Scott, twenty-eight, sported a three-day stubble.

"I'm not making a fashion statement," he explained. "I just haven't had the time to shave."

"A lot of young guys don't shave because they think women like the rugged look," I said.

"I know," Scott said. "They're trying to be hip. But a real man wakes up every morning and shaves. Tomorrow I'll get rid of this stubble."

"I got rid of mine this morning," I said.

"You're a real man," said Scott, who directed me to The Art of Shaving, where I spoke with manager Linda Wheeless.

"These young guys think they started the trend, but it originated with Crockett and Tubbs," she said, referring to the characters played by Don Johnson and Philip Michael Thomas on the 1980s cop show "Miami Vice."

"It wasn't even cool then," I said. "And it looks really dumb on these young guys today, especially the ones who get all dressed up but don't shave."

"It makes them look unkempt," Linda said.

"I like to look kempt," I replied. "My wife appreciates it, too."

Linda, whose son shaves not just his face but his head and whose grandson is too young to shave, showed me a picture of her husband, Richard, a handsome guy with a beard.

"He keeps it neat," she said. "No stubble. I wouldn't like that."

Then she showed me one of the most popular items in the store, a trimmer that can be set to help guys keep a perpetual stubble.

"Why don't they just use it to shave?" I asked.

"I don't know," Linda answered. "As long as they buy it, I don't care."

The next day, after I used my trusty twin-blade razor, I snuggled up to Sue again.

"How does that feel?" I asked.

"Much better," she said. "Nice and smooth."

It was, of course, a close shave.

"The Inn Crowd"

If I can afford to retire when I am eligible — I took a vow of poverty when I went into journalism, so I may be working posthumously — I'd like to be an innkeeper.

Sue, who is a teacher, thinks it's a great idea — that I retire, not that I continue to work even after I am dead — because she'd like to quit, too.

Then we can be like Bob Newhart and Mary Frann, who played the husband-and-wife owners of a Vermont bed and breakfast that was frequented by kooky characters on the old TV sitcom "Newhart."

To B&B or not to B&B — that is the question Sue and I have been asking ourselves. To find the answer, I spoke with Neil Carr, eighty-three, a lovable character who owns the Sea Beach Inn in Hyannis, Massachusetts, where Sue and I stayed when we spent a very pleasant weekend on Cape Cod.

"I love people — that's why I am in this place," Neil told me. "You have to have a positive outlook."

"Do you ever get any kooky characters here?" I asked.

"You mean like you?" Neil responded.

"Yes," I said.

Neil chuckled and said, "You're not kooky. In fact, you're normal compared to some of the guests I've had. One of them is here right now."

He was referring to an exceedingly fussy woman who had traveled from Missouri to watch her daughter play in a field hockey tournament.

"She's a pain in the butt," Neil explained. "She wants bacon and eggs every morning. I told her that we serve only a continental breakfast. She said, 'Is that all I'm getting?' I said, 'That's it, honey.' She's also been driving the cleaning girls crazy. One of them came down and said, 'What's going on in Room Two?' I said, 'She's here for six days. It's good money. Humor her.' That lady has been avoiding me and I've been avoiding her.

And where's her poor husband? Back home. He's probably been drunk since she left."

Neil has also had his share of crazy adventures since he and his late wife, Elizabeth, bought the Sea Beach Inn in 1987.

"About ten years ago I decided to add a prefabricated garage with a room on top," Neil recalled. "I had a spot cleared off and the footings put in. Then I got a call from a guy on Route 6 who said he had this building in a big dump truck. Part of the building brought a wire down, so now I had the cops on my hands. This guy was a terrible driver. He had to turn the truck around in a parking lot and come down the street, and there was traffic piling up behind him as far as you could see, and it looked like he was going to wreck the lawn of the people across the street. The woman who owned the house used to own the inn. She sold it to me. So now she wanted to kill me. She said, 'Now you can look down into my living room.' I said, 'Who'd want to look at you anyway?' She moved into a condo, but I hear she's still alive. She must be ninety-eight. She used to pop out from behind trees. She could have been in a cartoon."

"Or," I added, "a sitcom."

"This is just the place for one," said Neil.

"Would you ever sell the inn?" I inquired.

"One couple recently asked me that," Neil replied. "They followed me around. The wife said, 'This must be a wonderful life for you. We'd like to get a B&B.' I said, 'Really? I'll tell you what. I'll call the bank and find out what I still owe them. You go upstairs and get your checkbook. Pay me for what I still owe on the place, add two dollars to it and I'll be out by five o'clock this afternoon.'"

"Maybe my wife and I will buy it when we retire," I said. "Until then, we'll come back as guests."

"You and your wife are always welcome," Neil said. "I could talk to you until the cows come home. We don't have any cows, but two horses used to live here. They could have been in the sitcom, too."

"Spaced Out"

I didn't major in physics in college, though I do have a BS in life, but I know that one of the principles of this fascinating science is that any space will be filled — except, of course, the one between my ears.

So it is no surprise that practically every nook and cranny of my house is filled with stuff. This includes drawers I can barely open because they are crammed with things like pots, pans, pot holders, hot plates, sandwich bags, aluminum foil, socks, T-shirts, pajamas, sweaters, sweatshirts, sweatpants, and underwear. The sandwich bags and the underwear are not, you should know, in the same drawer.

A couple of closets are bursting with coats, jackets, windbreakers, and parkas, most of which aren't mine.

Then there are containers spilling over with pens and pencils and a large receptacle loaded with spatulas, potato mashers, soup ladles, and wooden spoons. If I even tried to fit a toothpick in there, the whole thing would explode.

One cabinet is jammed with dozens of pieces of Tupperware, which I could swear are engaging in intimate activities and are reproducing at such an alarming rate that when I open the doors, half of them rain down on my head. It's a good thing we don't keep crockery up there.

I could buy a barrel the size of a Volkswagen in which to store paper clips and within a week it will be filled to overflowing.

And don't even get me started on the garage, which is filled with too many things to mention, much of them belonging to Katie and Lauren, who don't live at home anymore. The one thing that's not in the garage is a car.

To find an explanation for this frightening phenomenon, I called Alain Brizard, a professor of physics at my alma mater, Saint Michael's College in Colchester, Vermont.

"There is a saying in physics that nature abhors a vacuum," Brizard told me.

"I abhor a vacuum, too," I replied. "It's in one of the closets with all those coats and jackets. I can't even close the door."

"That's because of the second law of thermodynamics," said the good professor.

This law states that the entropy of an isolated system never decreases. Entropy, according to Brizard, is a sense or measure of disorder.

"Teens and toddlers are masters of entropy," said Brizard, noting that his seventeen-year-old son, Peter, an otherwise fine and upstanding young man, is a prime example.

"His room is filled with stuff," the professor told me. "There are clothes all over the floor. If there is a piece of the floor that is exposed, it will soon be covered with clothes. The only spot that isn't covered with clothes is covered by the bed."

While entropy could be blamed for the disorder in Peter's room, another scientific explanation is that he is a chip off the old building block of matter.

"My office is a mess," Brizard confessed. "There are papers all over the floor. But if you ask me for a specific piece of paper, I will find it. Chaos is not all that it seems. Sometimes there is order in chaos."

Brizard's wife, Dinah, a professional chef whose kitchen is spotless ("I help by doing the dishes," Brizard said), and Sue, a teacher and a fellow St. Mike's grad, are both orderly.

"This must fall under the first law of marriage: Opposites attract," I said.

Brizard agreed, adding: "Entropy can be defeated. One way is to clean out your drawers and closets once in a while. But the best way is to be married to someone who is orderly."

For this theory alone, Prof. Brizard deserves to win the Nobel Prize. I just hope he can find it under all those papers in his office.

"College Daze"

As soon as my lawyer gets out of jail, I am going to file a classless action lawsuit against the makers of "National Lampoon's Animal House" for theft of intellectual property.

I came up with the idea recently while drinking a beer at my fortieth college reunion, where my classmates (who also, like my lawyer, were admitted to the bar) agreed that the 1978 campus comedy was heavily influenced by our shenanigans.

While we got an excellent education at Saint Michael's College, which is annually rated as one of the top small colleges in America, the Class of 1975 stands out as the most notorious in the 111-year history of the school.

That its graduates, like those in "Animal House," have gone on to enjoy distinguished careers in business, education, law, politics, medicine, aviation, and even journalism only bolsters my case.

The plaintiffs, whose last names are not being used to protect the guilty, include Hank, my roommate for three years; Clay, my roommate for one year; Tim, the brazen ringleader who lived next door; and yours truly, who was only, I will testify under oath in the event we are countersued, along for the ride.

Accompanying us to the reunion were Hank's wife, Angela; Clay's wife, Lorraine; Tim's wife, Jane; and Sue, who also is a member of the Class of '75 but is innocent of all charges, unless you count being guilty by association.

The first thing Tim and I did, with help from Clay, was turn the Class of 1975 banner upside down on a fence in back of the school. It hung proudly, if slightly crumpled, next to the crisp, right-side-up banners of the other classes at the reunion barbecue. Then the three of us, along with several of our classmates, posed for pictures behind it.

Tim, co-chair of the '75 reunion committee, later reported that Jack Neuhauser, who has been president of the college since 2007 but knows all about us, heard what we had done.

"He just shook his head, like he expected it," Tim said.

"He can't revoke our diplomas," I noted, adding that we graduated magna cum lager, "or we'd have to come back."

"And repeat all the stuff we did," said Tim.

That stuff included starting a snowball fight that erupted into a campus-wide riot; putting snakes in other students' rooms; engaging in firecracker wars; throwing a burning bonsai tree out of a window and accidentally igniting the ivy on the side of the building, which forced our resident adviser, Flash, to run across the quad, beer in hand, to extinguish the blaze; locking a pep squad in a dormitory basement so it couldn't march at a pep rally; putting kegs of beer in a dumbwaiter and sending them up and down between floors so campus authorities couldn't find them; streaking in front of the girls' dorm (I did, modestly, wear a bow tie); creating an international incident on a trip to Montreal; and committing innumerable other acts of mayhem, craziness, and blatant stupidity that are safe to mention now because, let's hope, the statute of limitations has expired.

"The drinking age was eighteen," Tim reasoned. "What did they expect?"

They expected us to behave ourselves at the reunion, which we did. Mostly.

At the awards breakfast (somehow, none of us won anything), I issued a blanket apology for the Class of 1975 to the now-retired Don "Pappy"

Sutton, who was dean of students during our four-year reign of error, when Playboy ranked St. Mike's as one of the nation's top party schools.

Dean Sutton, who is eighty-seven and looks fabulous (he's had forty years to recover), thanked me and said, "God bless you."

We had a great time, both in college and at the reunion, and are proud to be associated with such a fine institution of higher learning.

I can't help but think, however, that like the rowdy crew in "Animal House," we are still on double secret probation.

CHAPTER 17

"Chloe Meets Santa"

In 1897, which was before my time (six a.m. is before my time, too, but that's another story), a little girl named Virginia asked if there was a Santa Claus.

In 2015, a little girl named Chloe got up at six a.m. in her grandparents' house and asked for breakfast. Then she asked if there was a Santa Claus.

She found out when she went to the Smith Haven Mall in Lake Grove, New York, to see the right jolly old elf who made her laugh when she saw him in spite of herself.

As a sometimes naughty boy who is trying to get on the good list so I can receive reindeer underwear for Christmas, I am not lying when I say that this Santa is the best I have ever seen.

His real name is Ernest Johnson. But he is known in holiday circles, which look remarkably like wreaths, as Santa Ernie.

"I love being Santa Claus," he told me in a phone conversation a couple of weeks before meeting Chloe.

Santa Ernie has greeted good little boys and girls at Smith Haven every year since 2001. But he took the role long before that, in 1979, at the age of forty.

"I told a little girl four years ago that I was six hundred and fifty-four, which makes me six hundred and fifty-eight now," Santa Ernie said.

"You don't sound a day over four hundred and eighty-three," I replied.

He chuckled and said, "Being Santa Claus keeps me young."

When Chloe and I met him, he certainly looked the part. His droll little mouth was drawn up like a bow, and the beard on his chin was as white as the snow. He had a broad face and a little round belly that shook when he laughed like a bowl full of jelly.

"Hello, Chloe!" he said cheerily, his blue eyes twinkling behind round spectacles.

"Santa!" exclaimed Chloe, who will be three in March. She was accompanied by Sue, Lauren, Guillaume, and, of course, yours truly.

Chloe wore a red Christmas dress, with a gift-box bow in her blond curls.

"You're beautiful, sweetheart!" Santa Ernie told her.

"Say thank you," Lauren said.

"Thank you," said Chloe, who wandered through the Santa's Village display in the center of the mall. She had the place to herself because our special visit was arranged by Noerr Programs, a family and holiday services company headquartered not at the North Pole but in Arvada, Colorado, which gets plenty of snow, too.

One of Santa Ernie's helpers gave Chloe a little stuffed husky, which presumably helps pull the sleigh if Dasher or Dancer, or Prancer or Vixen, or Comet or Cupid, or Donner or Blitzen calls in sick.

Chloe clutched the dog as she sat with Santa Ernie and Lauren for a picture, but she wanted to do more exploring, so a very helpful elf gave her a book, which she promptly opened and put in front of her face, making the photographer's job a tad challenging.

Santa Ernie, who with his wife of fifty-five years has two children, three grandchildren, and three great-grandchildren, and has greeted thousands of boys and girls over the years, knew just what to do to make the picture perfect.

At the end of her visit, Chloe hugged Santa Ernie and gave him a high-five.

"Say thank you to Santa," Lauren said.

"Thank you, Santa," Chloe said, adding sweetly, "I love you."

"Merry Christmas, Chloe!" Santa Ernie said.

"Merry Christmas!" she responded with a wide smile, knowing full well the magical answer to that age-old question:

Yes, Chloe, there is a Santa Claus.

"Picasso Baby's Room"

The day Sue and I found out we were going to be grandparents, Lauren informed me that I had a job.

"You have to paint," she said.

"I told Mom I'm retired from painting," I replied. "She wants me to do the hallway."

"Not your house," Lauren said. "Our house. You have to paint the baby's room."

Writing this book has brought back memories of how it all began, three years ago, when I prepared for Chloe's arrival by painting the room that would be hers.

As a painter, Pablo Picasso had nothing on me. Sure, he had a Blue Period, but it lasted only three years. My Blue Period has lasted more than ten times that long, and every time I've had a painting project, it's made me blue, which is the color of the master bedroom and the adjoining bathroom.

It's also made me green (downstairs bathroom), yellow (upstairs bathroom), white (family room), sea foam (hallway), and rose (living room and dining room, which puts me one up on Picasso's Rose Period).

When I announced to Sue that I was retired from painting, she said, "You're not retired. You're just on hiatus."

My hiatus ended when Lauren asked me to paint the baby's room.

I had haunting flashbacks to my many painting misadventures. Like the time I painted the kitchen in the condo where Sue, Katie, Lauren, and I lived in our hometown of Stamford before we moved to Long Island. The trickiest part was painting around the ceiling fan, where the lights were situated. I worked with the lights on until I smelled something burning. It was my hair, which had come in contact with a hot bulb. I pulled one of two cords — the one I thought would turn off the lights — only to discover that I had turned on the fan, whereupon a whirling blade hit me in the head.

It should have knocked some sense into me, but I kept on with the painting projects, including a particularly awful one in the living room of our house, which had huge ceiling beams that Sue wanted me to remove. I initially used a crowbar that punched holes in the ceiling. Then I used a rope to yank the beams down. One narrowly missed my skull. It took me a week to complete the project.

Fortunately, when it came time to paint the baby's room, I got help from Guillaume, who was embarking on his first painting project.

I told him that the worst part of painting isn't the painting, it's the prep work. This includes using a mile and a half of masking tape to cover areas you don't want to paint. Then you have to prime the walls and the ceiling. When you paint, you have to put on two coats, though if it's a hot day, you can wear a T-shirt.

The good thing about the project in the baby's room was that we didn't have to paint the ceiling. And Guillaume bought a new kind of paint that contained primer. Also, the walls needed only one coat.

The best part was that Guillaume proved to be a natural.

"When I painted for the first time," I told him, "I barely knew which end of the brush to use."

"It could have been a brush with disaster," he replied.

"I am so proud of you!" I exclaimed, knowing this project would be enjoyable because I'd be sharing it with a fellow punster. "This is going to pan out."

"We can put it on our bucket list," said Guillaume.

"It's a good thing our wives aren't here," I said. "They'd bristle at our jokes."

"Yes," Guillaume responded, "but we're on a roll."

It went on like this for most of the day. When Sue and Lauren got back from shopping for baby clothes, they marveled at the nice work we did and approved of the light pink color, which Lauren chose because she knew she was having a girl.

And what a girl she has turned out to be, a precious sweetheart who fills our lives with love and joy and who sleeps in the pretty pink room that Daddy and Poppie painted.

Picasso couldn't have done a better job.

Epilogue

"Poppie's Letter to Chloe"

Dear Chloe:

You have always loved books. This one is for you.

Even when you were a baby, you wanted Mommy, Daddy, or Nini to read to you. But you especially loved it when I did. I loved it, too. I still do.

Now that you are beginning to read on your own, and will continue to read through a lifetime of loving books, I wanted to show you what I am sure you already know: How crazy your Poppie is — and how crazy I am for you.

We have already done a lot of fun things, many of them chronicled in this book. And we will do plenty more, even as the years roll on, and you develop other interests, and meet new people, and eventually make a life of your own.

Through it all, remember how lucky you are to have Mommy and Daddy, who have raised you with life's two most important gifts: love and laughter.

Remember also how much Nini loves you and does fun things with you, too. Same goes for Aunt Katie and Uncle Dave.

And remember how special you are to me, and how my love for you is limitless, and how much I look forward to our next adventure.

I'll see you soon, Honey. I can't wait!

Love always,
Poppie

Printed in the United States
By Bookmasters